LEON

HAPPY ONE-POT COOKING

BY REBECCA SEAL & JOHN VINCENT

conran
OCTOPUS

CONTENTS

INTRODUCTION

We think of one-pot cooking as one joyous legal rave. A flavour party with a happy crowd of diverse ingredients, tastes and goodness.

There is a Hindu story that pictures the universe as a web of jewels, all interconnected with string. Each jewel has its own brilliance but also reflects and refracts the brilliance of all the other jewels. Each jewel enhances the whole. That is how we think about one-pot cooking.

We have written this book to make it easier for everyone to eat well. It is why we started LEON. We do that in our restaurants, and we look to do that with our books. In both, we put flavour first, and marry it with goodness.

Putting everything into one pot, and letting the alchemy happen while you are watching Game of Thrones, eating scones or on your phone, makes everything a whole lot simpler. And it makes the washing-up easier too. You can even stick the cooking pot on the table (but obviously put a LEON × John Lewis heat protector down first).

Enjoy the variety. We've tried to spread our culinary wings wide with this book and take you to many places. We hope you love both the journey and the destination.

Thank you so much for buying this book. There is a whole lot of love and work in here. We hope that it comes across in the flavours.

Please enjoy the party.

Rebecca & John xxx

KEY

WF
WHEAT FREE

GF
GLUTEN FREE

DF
DAIRY FREE

V
VEGETARIAN

Ve
VEGAN

STORECUPBOARD

FRIDGE

lemongrass
ginger
spring onions
fresh chillies
tofu

thick plain yoghurt
coconut yoghurt
Parmesan
ready-rolled all-butter puff pastry
feta

goats' cheese
mozzarella
double cream
fresh gnocchi
smoked mackerel

FREEZER

peas
lime leaves
sweetcorn
chopped spinach
wheat or corn tortillas
home-made stock
bacon or pancetta
Indian flatbreads
chorizo

VEGETABLES, FRUIT & HERBS

garlic
onions
shallots
leeks
basil
coriander
parsley
chives
rosemary

tarragon
thyme
oranges
lemons
limes
spring greens
hispi cabbage
sweet potatoes

NUTS & SEEDS

flaked & chopped almonds
pine nuts
pumpkin seeds

roasted sesame seeds
roasted unsalted peanuts

MISCELLANEOUS

fish sauce	red wine vinegar
coconut milk	mirin
passata	preserved lemons
soy sauce	microwaveable rice
anchovies	dried black olives
flaky sea salt	capers in brine
ready-cooked noodles	tomato purée
glass noodles	breadcrumbs
maple syrup	extra virgin olive oil
tamarind paste	oil for cooking
chermoula paste	kimchi
harissa paste	eggs
roasted red pepper paste	
roasted red peppers	
sriracha	

PULSES & GRAINS

red lentils
pearl barley
cooked Puy lentils
cooked green lentils
cooked chickpeas
basmati & wild rice mix
cooked black beans
cooked freekeh
basmati rice
risotto rice
quinoa

SPICES

ground cumin	saffron	dried chillies
ground coriander	cayenne	curry powder
cardamom pods	nutmeg	curry leaves
ground turmeric	mustard seeds	garam masala
ground cinnamon	fennel seeds	
smoked & sweet paprika	chilli flakes	

TIPS & TRICKS

CHOOSE YOUR STARS

Every ingredient you use in a one-pot dish needs to earn its place, so make the most of things that are really punchy – like spiced, fermented tofu, fiery chillies, garlic, ginger, lemongrass, good-quality spices or tangy cheeses. Bonus points if that flavour comes in a tiny package, like teeny, mouth-puckering capers or umami-rich anchovies. Try to buy ethically produced and sustainably sourced meat, fish, eggs and dairy as, not only is it kinder to the planet, but it'll be tastier too. One-pot cooking may be simple, but there's no place for bland food in our kitchen.

Fresh herbs are your friends. They instantly add zing and will round out any meal, even one you've scratched together in a corner-shop trolley-dash. If you can, keep a collection of soft herb plants going on your windowsill – mint, basil, parsley and coriander – with hardier rosemary, bay, chives, thyme and marjoram in pots outside.

TIME IS OF THE ESSENCE

When you want to cook quickly, spring onions will give a sweet allium kick, without the need to slowly sauté and soften onions and with less intensity than garlic. Garlic cloves can be blanched in a mug of boiling water to quickly pull flavour into your dish without overpowering it.

Keep ready-made pastes or sauces, such as North African chermoula, harissa or Korean gochujang, in the fridge. Slather them on meat, fish or vegetables and sling into the oven for a super-easy but high-impact meal.

IMPROMPTU COOKING

For those moments when we need a speedy meal with minimal washing-up, we keep a stash of ready-cooked pulses like Puy lentils, black beans and chickpeas, in jars, pouches or tins, as well as microwaveable rice and even freekeh (toasted green wheat). If you've got flatbreads in the freezer, and dried pasta on a shelf, you'll never be far from a good, tasty, impromptu dinner.

LOVE YOUR POTS & PANS

HABITS TO LAST A LIFETIME

We confess. We're not perfect when it comes to caring for our pots and pans. Who is? Sometimes the only spoon to hand is metal and we end up dragging it over a non-stick pan. We've chucked cast-iron into the dishwasher and had to scrape day-old, charcoaled remnants off a baking dish. But we're mending our ways, because cookware can last a lifetime if you care for it properly.

When cooking, pure oils and fats (rather than margarines or cooking sprays) won't leave a sticky build-up over time. Slowly heat the pan first, then add fat – this makes food less likely to stick, as does letting food come to room temperature before adding it to the pan.

HAND-WASHING IS BEST

While dishwashers are dreamy for crocks and cutlery, they aren't the best for pots, pans and sharp knives. Non-stick, metal and enamel can all be damaged by their abrasive cleaning, so for a long and happy life together, hand-wash cooking pans in hot soapy water with a non-scratch sponge scourer. Never drop a just-used, piping hot pan into water though; the change in temperature can warp the metal and it will never sit flat again.

Rather than soaking burnt-on food, it is better for the pan to add a little water and bring it to a simmer, then scrape the crusty bits with a wooden spoon or heatproof spatula as though de-glazing for a sauce.

After washing, any pan which isn't non-stick will be pleased to get a dose of moisturizer in the form of neutral cooking oil before being put away. Dab a little oil on to kitchen paper, then wipe a very thin layer all over the cooking surface. You can also 'season' cast-iron pans by heating on the stove, then repeatedly wiping a thin layer of oil over the metal in the same way. Do this for 10 minutes or so, to increase the pan's non-stick-ability and preserve its finish.

NATURALLY FAST

MAKE A HASH OF THIS

SERVES 2

PREP TIME: 5 MINS • COOK TIME: 25 MINS

WF • GF (check sausage ingredients) • DF

250g **Maris Piper potatoes**, peeled and diced into rough 2cm pieces

150g **cooking chorizo**, diced into rough 2cm pieces

1 tablespoon **olive oil**

4 **eggs**

TO SERVE:

2 **spring onions**, finely chopped

finely chopped fresh coriander or **parsley**

finely chopped **green chilli** (optional)

There's no shame in eating this straight from the pan…

Start by par-cooking the potatoes in the microwave – this step isn't essential (so don't worry if you don't have a microwave) but it helps the outside of the potato to crisp up in the pan. Place in a bowl with a tablespoon of water, cover and microwave on full for 3 minutes. Drain thoroughly.

Meanwhile place a medium-sized frying pan over a medium heat. Add the diced chorizo and, once the fat starts to run, add the potatoes and the olive oil. Turn the heat down to low and cook, stirring and turning everything frequently, for 15–20 minutes, until the potato pieces are crisp on the outside and cooked within. If the meat begins to char, remove it from the pan and set aside while the potatoes finish cooking.

Make 4 wells in the chorizo and potato mixture and break an egg into each one. Cook until done to your liking, around 4 minutes. Tilt the pan slightly and scoop up spoonfuls of the hot fat to pour over the top of each egg if you like the whites to be well cooked.

Serve garnished with the chopped spring onions, herbs and chilli, if using.

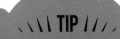

\\\\ TIP ////

Make this an even more filling meal by adding cooked chickpeas to the pan a couple of minutes before adding the eggs.

JANSSON'S TEMPTATION

SERVES 3–4
PREP TIME: 15 MINS • COOK TIME: 1 HOUR 10 MINS

30g **salted butter**

1 large **white onion**, very finely sliced
(use a mandolin if possible)

750g **potatoes**, cut into ½cm matchsticks

200g **pickled herrings**, drained
and torn into 5cm × 2cm pieces

400–450ml **whipping cream**

2 tablespoons **breadcrumbs**

salt and **freshly ground black pepper**

rye bread and **butter**, to serve

SALAD:

2 tablespoons **extra virgin olive oil**

1 tablespoon **freshly squeezed**
lemon juice

300g mixture of **bitter salad**
leaves (chicory, endive, frisée,
radicchio, mizuna, watercress)

flaky sea salt

This Swedish baked fish, cream and potato dish is usually served as part of a smörgåsbord, or celebratory meal. If you like, you can serve it with some dark Scandinavian-style rye bread and butter, as well as salad.

Don't make it with anchovies – Swedish recipes call for ansjovis, which is often mistranslated. The original recipe is made with pickled sprats, which you should use if you can find them. We find that pickled herrings are easier to come by in the UK, so we usually make it that way, instead.

Heat the oven to 160°C/325°F/gas mark 3.

Place a wide ovenproof pan over a medium heat. Add the butter and, when melted, add the onions, potatoes and a pinch of salt. Allow both to soften, cooking gently, for about 10 minutes. Don't allow to brown – turn the heat down if necessary.

Remove from the heat and tuck the herring pieces evenly throughout the mixture. Pour over the whipping cream, using only as much as is necessary to just submerge the potatoes. Spread the mixture out so it sits fairly neatly in the pan, and make sure all the herring pieces are out of sight under the cream. Season well with lots of black pepper and scatter over the breadcrumbs.

Place in the preheated oven and cook for 50–60 minutes, or until the potato is tender (use a sharp knife to check this in several places in the pan). Meanwhile make the salad: whisk together the olive oil, lemon juice and a pinch of salt to make a dressing and, just before serving, toss through the leaves.

Serve hot or warm, with the salad on the side.

\\\ TIP ///
Jansson's temptation makes a delicious side to go with sausages, meatballs or lamb.

BAKED GNOCCHI

SERVES 4

PREP TIME: 5 MINS • COOK TIME: 25 MINS, plus 5 mins standing

WF • GF (check gnocchi ingredients) • V

250ml **vegetable stock**

500g **fresh gnocchi**

150g **broccoli**, cut into small florets

100g **blue cheese**

200ml **double cream**

freshly ground black pepper

A soothing dish for a cold, wintry evening, ready within 45 minutes of getting through your front door.

Heat the oven to 200°C/400°F/gas mark 6.

An ovenproof frying pan, measuring about 25cm across, is ideal for this dish. Set it over a medium heat and add the stock. When boiling, add the gnocchi – the liquid won't cover them. Cook for a couple of minutes, turning the gnocchi in the stock, to start the cooking process.

Remove from the heat and add the broccoli to the pan, then crumble in the blue cheese. Pour over the cream and stir gently to distribute everything evenly, making sure the broccoli is coated in the creamy sauce.

Finish with a good dose of black pepper (the gnocchi and the cheese will add enough salt on their own) and slide into the preheated oven. Cook for 20 minutes, or until the top of the dish is just turning to a light gold colour.

Leave to stand for 5 minutes before serving.

\\\\ TIP ////

For a bit of crunch, sprinkle the top with chopped walnuts 5 minutes before the end of cooking.

PEA, FETA & DILL FRITTATA

SERVES 2

PREP TIME: 10 MINS • COOK TIME: 5 MINS

WF • GF • V

2 teaspoons **olive oil**

4 **eggs**

1 **spring onion**, finely chopped, or
1 tablespoon **chopped fresh chives**

1 teaspoon **finely chopped fresh parsley**

1 tablespoon **finely chopped fresh dill**

75g **frozen peas**, defrosted (cover in
boiling water to hurry this up
if necessary)

50g **feta**, crumbled

salt and **freshly ground black pepper**

A frittata is a flat Italian omelette, and can be made with all sorts of fridge-raider fillings. It makes an excellent home-late-can't-be-bothered-to-cook kind of meal.

Set a medium frying pan (ours is 25cm across) over a low heat and pour in the oil. Heat the grill.

Crack the eggs into a bowl and season with a little salt (the feta will be salty) and lots of black pepper. Beat very lightly – over-mixing can give the omelette a spongy texture. Add the rest of the ingredients, mix once to combine, then carefully pour into the hot pan. Cook until the egg is pulling away from the edges, about 4 minutes, but runny on the top. Slide the pan under the hot grill and cook for 1 minute, just enough to set the egg.

Place a plate over the pan and flip, so that the golden underside of the frittata is uppermost, to serve. Slice and eat hot or at room temperature.

\\\\ TIP ////
Customize your frittata by adding good-quality canned or smoked fish, leftover cooked vegetables – especially potatoes – or roast meats, cheese, ham or cooked sausage.

CHOP, CHOP!

SERVES 2

PREP TIME: 8 MINS · COOK TIME: 15 MINS

WF · GF · DF

2 tablespoons **olive oil**

2 large or 4 small **lamb chops**,
   at room temperature

2 cloves of **garlic**, bruised

1 sprig of **fresh rosemary**

1 × 400g can of **cannellini beans**,
   drained and rinsed

200g **hispi cabbage (sweetheart** or
   pointed cabbage), finely shredded

2 tablespoons **finely chopped
   fresh parsley**

salt and **freshly ground black pepper**

Juicy chops and garlicky beans, ready in less than 25 minutes.

Place a large frying pan over a high heat and add a splash of the oil. Season the chops all over with salt and pepper, and when the pan is very hot, cook for a couple of minutes each side, until medium, or to your taste.

Remove the chops and set aside to rest; keep warm. Meanwhile add the rest of the oil to the pan along with the garlic and rosemary. After a couple of minutes, as the garlic releases its flavour into the oil, add the beans and hispi cabbage to the pan and sauté gently for 3 or 4 minutes, stirring, until the beans are warmed through and the cabbage has wilted. Remove from the heat and stir in the parsley. Taste to check the seasoning – the beans will probably need a little salt.

Remove the garlic cloves and serve the cabbage and bean mixture alongside the lamb chops.

TIP

This bean and cabbage mixture also works beautifully with pork chops, pork sausages or merguez.

PAD THAI

SERVES 2

PREP TIME: 10 MINS • COOK TIME: 10 MINS

WF · GF · DF

1 teaspoon **tamarind concentrate**

1 tablespoon **soft brown sugar**
or **palm sugar**

1½ tablespoons **fish sauce**

100g **dried sen lek (Thai folded rice noodles)**

vegetable oil

150g **extra firm tofu**, cut into cubes

2 **shallots**, finely sliced

75g **raw shelled prawns**

1 **egg**

a good pinch of **chilli powder**

75g **bean sprouts**, reserving a few to garnish

2 **spring onions**, very finely chopped, reserving a little to garnish

TO SERVE:

25g crushed roasted **unsalted peanuts**

lime wedges

\\\ TIP ///

When frying tofu, it will initially stick but should become easier to turn after a little more cooking.

Pad Thai (or phat Thai) was popularized by Thai prime minister Plaek Pibulsonggram – nicknamed Phibun – in the 1940s, as part of his campaign to unify the ethnically diverse country and promote cheap, nutritious food. It worked – not only is pad Thai the country's national dish, but it is loved worldwide. It should be tangy, salty and slightly sweet, with soft noodles and crunchy nuts.

Sen lek (folded rice noodles) are available in larger supermarkets, as are bottles of tamarind concentrate.

Whisk together the tamarind concentrate, sugar and fish sauce with 1½ tablespoons of boiling water, until the sugar has dissolved.

Soak the noodles in more boiling water for 8 minutes (or soak according to the packet instructions), until just al dente. While soaking, move the noodles around so that they are less likely to stick together. Drain well.

Set a wok over a high heat and pour in about ½cm of vegetable oil. When hot, slide in the tofu and shallots. Cook for about 5 minutes, gently turning the tofu once browned underneath, until both are golden brown – don't let them catch or burn, as they will become bitter. Remove the wok from the heat and use a slotted spoon to lift them out, then set aside. Carefully spoon off half the oil and discard.

Have ready all of the other ingredients: break the egg into a small bowl or cup and measure out everything else.

When ready to cook, place the wok back on the heat. When hot again, return the shallots and tofu to the pan, along with the drained noodles, prawns and egg. Stir continuously for about a minute, breaking up the egg, then add 2 tablespoons of the tamarind sauce, the chilli powder, and most of the bean sprouts and spring onions. Stir-fry for another minute, then taste and add more of the sauce, if necessary.

Serve garnished with the rest of the bean sprouts and spring onions and the crushed peanuts, with a wedge of lime to squeeze over. Eat straight away.

ONE-PAN MARJORAM PASTA

SERVES 2

PREP TIME: 5 MINS • COOK TIME: 12 MINS

V

500ml good-quality **vegetable** or **chicken stock**

200g **orecchiette**

5 tablespoons **double cream**

1 clove of **garlic**, bruised

2 tablespoons **pine nuts**

2 tablespoons **roughly chopped fresh marjoram**, plus a little more to garnish

freshly ground black pepper

This has to be one of our favourite one-pot discoveries: cooking dried pasta in stock, which then becomes the pasta's sauce. Starch from the pasta combines with the stock as you stir it, turning it into a light but silky sauce. This flavour combination is thanks to the food writer Katie Caldesi, who writes brilliantly about Italian food.

Place a saucepan over a medium heat and add the stock. When boiling, add the pasta. Bring back up to the boil, then cover and turn the heat right down. Cook until the pasta is about half done, or very al dente, stirring every couple of minutes — because there isn't as much liquid as with a normal pan of pasta, there is more risk of it sticking to itself or the pan.

Add the cream and the garlic to the pan and stir well, then replace the lid and cook for another couple of minutes, stirring once or twice again, until the pasta is al dente. Remove from the heat and add lots of black pepper, the pine nuts and fresh marjoram.

Taste to check the seasoning — because of the stock you almost certainly won't need any salt. If the sauce seems too thick or dry, loosen it with a little hot water. Remove the garlic clove before serving. Top each bowlful with a little more marjoram.

\ \ \ \ **TIP** / / / /

If you can't find fresh marjoram, use fresh oregano or even fresh basil instead. Or swap it for a couple of tablespoons of ready-made roasted red pepper paste.

\\\\\|||////

QUESADILLAS
4 WAYS

Mexican quesadillas are stuffed and pan-fried tortillas, usually involving cheese, cooked in a dry pan until the filling melts and starts oozing from the sides.

If you need to avoid wheat, look out for soft corn tortillas (but check the ingredients, as some brands still contain wheat as well).

(Recipes overleaf)

4

1 ROAST PEPPER & REFRIED BEAN QUESADILLAS

SERVES 2 as a main course or 4 with other dishes
PREP TIME: 10 MINS • COOK TIME: 6 MINS per tortilla
V
. . . .

200g **roasted red peppers** from a jar, drained and
    chopped into 1cm pieces
200g **mature Cheddar**, coarsely grated
200g **refried beans** (about ½ a can)
6 tablespoons **roughly chopped fresh coriander**
2 **spring onions**, halved and finely chopped
2 teaspoons seeded and finely chopped **fresh red chilli**
1 heaped teaspoon **hot** or **sweet smoked paprika**
6 × 20cm **tortillas**

Mix everything apart from the tortillas together in a bowl. Divide into 6 roughly equal amounts.

Place a frying pan over a low–medium heat. When hot, place one of the tortillas in the pan and sprinkle one half of it with one sixth of the cheese mixture. Spread it evenly over half the tortilla, then fold the other half over it to make a half-moon shape. Cook for 2–3 minutes, until the bottom of the quesadilla is a light golden brown, then carefully flip and cook the other side. Remove from the pan and keep warm while you cook the rest. Cut each one in half to serve.

2 CORN & BLACK BEAN QUESADILLAS

SERVES 2 as a main course or 4 with other dishes
PREP TIME: 10 MINS • COOK TIME: 6 MINS per tortilla
V
. . . .

1 × 400g can of **cooked black beans**, drained and rinsed
    (approx. 230g drained weight)
100g **frozen sweetcorn**, defrosted (cover with boiling
    water to speed this up if necessary)
4 tablespoons **roughly chopped fresh coriander**
2 **spring onions**, halved and finely chopped
1 teaspoon **chipotle paste**, or more, to taste
juice of ½ **lime**
200g **mature Cheddar**, coarsely grated
6 × 20cm **tortillas**
a pinch of **salt**

Place the beans in a large bowl and mash a little with a fork.

Mix everything else, apart from the tortillas, into the beans. Divide into 6 roughly equal amounts, then cook as for the roast pepper & refried bean quesadillas, to the left, being careful not to overfill – the beans will spill out and the cheese will not melt if they are too thick. Cut each one in half to serve.

3 KIMCHI QUESADILLAS

SERVES 2 as a main course or 4 with other dishes
PREP TIME: 10 MINS • COOK TIME: 6 MINS per tortilla
V

. . . .

6 heaped tablespoons **kimchi**, drained and finely chopped

200g **mature Cheddar**, coarsely grated

6 tablespoons **roughly chopped fresh coriander**

2 **spring onions**, halved and finely chopped

6 × 20cm **tortillas**

Mix everything apart from the tortillas together in a bowl. Divide into 6 roughly equal amounts, then cook as for the roast pepper & refried bean quesadillas, on the opposite page. Cut each one in half to serve.

\\\\ TIP ////

Serve the quesadillas with guacamole and pico de gallo (and beer).

FOR THE GUACAMOLE: mash 1 ripe avocado with the juice of ½ a lime, 5 cherry tomatoes, seeded and finely chopped, 1 tablespoon of finely chopped seeded red chilli, 1 small shallot, very finely diced, 2 tablespoons of chopped coriander leaves and a pinch of salt.

FOR THE PICO DE GALLO: finely chop 2 shallots and 4 tomatoes, seeded, then add a squeeze of lime, some more chopped chilli, a pinch of salt and another 2 tablespoons of chopped coriander leaves.

4 CHEESY QUESADILLAS

SERVES 2 as a main course or 4 with other dishes
PREP TIME: 10 MINS • COOK TIME: 6 MINS per tortilla
V

. . . .

juice of ½ **lime**

200g **mature Cheddar**, coarsely grated

6 tablespoons **roughly chopped fresh coriander**

2 **spring onions**, halved and finely chopped

2 teaspoons seeded and finely chopped **fresh red chilli**

6 × 20cm **tortillas**

hot sauce, to serve (optional)

Mix together everything except the tortillas and hot sauce. Divide into 6 roughly equal amounts, then cook as for the roast pepper & refried bean quesadillas, on the opposite page.

Cut each one in half to serve, with hot sauce on the side if you like.

ROAST SALMON WITH ASPARAGUS & NEW POTATOES

SERVES 4

PREP TIME: 10 MINS • COOK TIME: 38 MINS

WF • GF • DF (check mayonnaise ingredients)

700g **new potatoes**, halved

1½ tablespoons **olive oil**

4 **salmon fillets**

400g **asparagus**, woody stems snapped off

zest of 1 **lemon**, reserving a pinch for the tartare sauce

salt and **freshly ground black pepper**

TARTARE SAUCE:

6 tablespoons **mayonnaise**

3 tablespoons **capers**, finely chopped

1 heaped tablespoon **finely chopped fresh dill**

a pinch of **lemon zest** (see above)

1 heaped tablespoon **finely chopped fresh parsley**

This is best made with in-season, locally grown asparagus, as it tastes better. Although quick and easy, it looks swish enough to serve at a dinner party.

Heat the oven to 200°C/400°F/gas mark 6.

Use a large metal baking dish. Toss the potatoes, oil, salt and pepper together, then slide into the preheated oven and cook for 30 minutes.

Pat the salmon fillets dry and season all over with salt and pepper. Place the asparagus in the baking dish and scatter over the lemon zest. Toss the vegetables gently, then top with the salmon, skin side up. Cook for 8 minutes, or until the salmon is cooked through and the asparagus is just done.

Meanwhile, mix the mayonnaise, capers, dill, a little lemon zest and the parsley together in a small serving bowl.

Serve the salmon and vegetables with the sauce.

\\\ TIP ///

For even more green goodness, swap out or add to the asparagus with snap peas, wedges of fennel, florets of tenderstem or purple sprouting broccoli.

ONE-PAN BACON & MUSHROOM PASTA

SERVES 2

PREP TIME: 10 MINS • COOK TIME: 20 MINS

DF (if using olive oil)

a knob of **butter** or a splash of **olive oil**

100g **smoked back bacon** or **pancetta**, finely chopped

200g **mixed mushrooms**, torn into bite-sized pieces – try **oyster** or **shiitake**

200g **medium-size pasta** (such as **rigatoni** or **fusilli**)

1 tablespoon **chopped fresh chives**

2 sprigs of **fresh thyme**, leaves only

freshly ground black pepper

Cooking the pasta in the same pan as the bacon and mushrooms means it absorbs their flavours, while the starch from the pasta thickens the cooking liquor to form a flavour-filled sauce.

Use a large wide pan with a lid. Set it over a medium heat and add the butter or olive oil. When hot, add the bacon or pancetta and sauté until crisp, stirring often so that it doesn't stick or burn.

Add the mushrooms to the pan and sauté until golden. Lift the mushrooms and bacon out of the pan and set to one side. Add 500ml boiling water, which will take on some colour from the pan, bring to a simmer, then add the pasta.

Cover and simmer for 6 minutes, stirring occasionally to prevent the pasta sticking. Remove the lid and turn up the heat to reduce the liquid, stirring often. After a couple of minutes, or once the pasta is al dente, remove from the heat. There should now be very little liquid left, just a silky reduction of pasta water. Return the mushrooms and bacon to the pan, and add the chives and thyme along with a generous amount of freshly ground black pepper. (Taste to check, but because of the bacon, you almost certainly won't need salt.) Stir well to allow the flavours to marry, and serve straight away.

\\\ **TIP** ///
This works very well without the meat, but will need a little salt or some Parmesan, added before serving.

SEA BASS WITH STICKY AUBERGINE & CHILLI

SERVES 4

PREP TIME: 10 MINS · COOK TIME: 40 MINS

WF · GF (check soy sauce ingredients) · DF

2 medium **aubergines** (about 500g)

2 tablespoons flavourless **cooking oil**, plus a little more for greasing

4 tablespoons **honey**

3cm piece of **fresh ginger**, peeled and grated

juice of 1 **lime**, plus 4 wedges to serve

4 tablespoons **dark soy sauce**

4 **sea bass fillets**

salt and **freshly ground black pepper**

TO SERVE:

2 teaspoons finely chopped **fresh red chilli**

2 **spring onions**, finely chopped

a handful of **fresh coriander leaves**

a pinch of toasted **sesame seeds**

Aubergine absorbs rich flavours brilliantly – here it soaks up the soy, honey and ginger until it becomes deliciously tangy, sticky and sweet. (Here's an added task: go online and try to work out whether the story of 'male and female' aubergines, and whether male taste better, is scientific fact or fiction.)

Heat the oven to 200°C/400°F/gas mark 6. Top and tail the aubergines, halve them through the middle, then cut into narrow, finger-sized wedges, trimming any very seedy bits off as you go. Grease a ceramic baking dish with a little cooking oil, then add the honey, ginger, lime juice, soy sauce and oil and mix until smooth. Add the aubergine pieces to the dish, toss thoroughly, then arrange in a single layer.

Slide the tray into the preheated oven and cook for 25–30 minutes, turning the aubergine once halfway through.

Taste a little of the aubergine to check if it is ready: it should be very tender, sticky, sweet and tangy. If it remains firm in the centre, return it to the oven for 5–10 minutes. Season the fish fillets, then place on top of the aubergine and return to the oven for 8 minutes.

To serve, lift the fish off the aubergine. Add half the chopped chilli and half the spring onions to the dish and toss. Place a portion of the sticky aubergine on each of 4 plates, then top each with a fish fillet. Serve scattered with the coriander leaves, a pinch of toasted sesame and the remaining spring onion and chilli, with a wedge of lime for squeezing over, on each plate.

\\\\ TIP ////

This is good with 200g of long green beans added to the baking dish at the same as the fish.

TURKISH-STYLE EGGS WITH YOGHURT & GREENS

SERVES 1
PREP TIME: 10 MINS • COOK TIME: 5 MINS

V

3 tablespoons **butter**

½ teaspoon **Turkish pul biber** or any **mild red pepper flakes**

100g **soft green cabbage**, **baby kale**, **spinach** or **chard**, hard stalks removed and leaves very finely shredded

1 clove of **garlic**, crushed

2 **eggs**

3 tablespoons **Greek-style yoghurt**, at room temperature if possible

1 sprig of **fresh dill**, finely chopped

a pinch of **salt**

hot buttered toast, to serve

This dish is based on cilbir, a Turkish poached egg and yoghurt dish. Pul biber is a mildly spiced, often salty, flaked red pepper, used as a condiment in Turkish cooking (find it in Middle Eastern stores and online). For cilbir, pul biber is mixed with melted butter to make a spiced, bright red sauce for the eggs. We've added greens, for both goodness and texture.

Put a small frying pan with a lid over a low heat and melt the butter in it. Spoon out about 2 tablespoons and mix with the pul biber flakes. Set aside. Place the pan back on the heat and add the shredded leaves and half the crushed garlic. Cook, stirring, for a couple of minutes, until the greens just begin to wilt. Make 2 wells in the greens, exposing the base of the pan, and break an egg into each one. Cover the pan so that the eggs cook quickly without the greens overdoing; cook until the eggs are done to your liking, 2–3 minutes.

Meanwhile stir together the yoghurt, remaining crushed garlic, salt and dill.

When the eggs are done, use a large spatula to lift them and the greens from the pan and on to a plate. Spoon over the garlic yoghurt, then drizzle the now bright red melted butter over everything. Eat straight away, with hot toast to dunk in the yolks and scoop up the garlicky, spicy sauce.

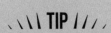

TIP

Room-temperature yoghurt is best for this dish, otherwise it will clash with the hot eggs and greens.

LEMONY PAN-BAKED MUSHROOMS & EGGS

SERVES 1
PREP TIME: 5 MINS · COOK TIME: 15 MINS
V

a knob of **butter**

300g **mushrooms** (chestnut or a mixture), sliced

2 sprigs of **fresh thyme**, leaves only, plus a little more to serve

1 clove of **garlic**, crushed

6 tablespoons **double cream**

2 teaspoons **lemon juice**

a pinch of **lemon zest**

1–2 **eggs**, depending on your hunger

salt and **freshly ground black pepper**

hot buttered toast, to serve

The cream makes this very simple supper (or brunch, or lunch) feel luxurious. You could even finish it off with a drop or two of truffle oil, if you happen to have some in the cupboard.

Place the butter in a small frying pan with a lid, set over a medium heat. Once melted, add the mushrooms and cook, stirring often, until lightly browned (if they leak a lot of water, spoon it off, as you don't want them to stew), about 6–8 minutes. Turn the heat right down and add the thyme leaves (reserving a little to garnish), garlic, salt and pepper. Stir, then add the cream, lemon juice and lemon zest. Cook for a minute. If it seems dry, add 1 tablespoon of water and mix.

Make 1–2 wells in the mushroom mixture, depending on the number of eggs you are using, and crack in the egg or eggs. Cover the pan and cook until the eggs are done to your liking, 2–3 minutes. Season the eggs with a little more salt and pepper.

Sprinkle with the reserved thyme and serve with hot buttered toast.

\\\ TIP ///

Add 100g of finely chopped fresh spinach to the pan and let it wilt down before adding the cream. For an even richer dish, add a little Taleggio cheese, cut into cubes, along with the eggs, or finish with a few shavings of Parmesan.

INDIAN-SPICED BAKED EGGS

SERVES 2
PREP TIME: 10 MINS • COOK TIME: 35 MINS
DF • V

1 tablespoon **cooking oil**

1 **onion**, finely diced

¼ teaspoon **ground cumin**

¼ teaspoon **mustard seeds**

¼ teaspoon **ground coriander**

¼ teaspoon **chilli flakes**

1 clove of **garlic**, crushed

1 teaspoon finely chopped **green chilli**

400g **cherry tomatoes**, halved

75g **frozen chopped spinach** (optional)

3 tablespoons **coconut milk** (optional)

2–4 **eggs**, depending on your hunger

salt and **freshly ground black pepper**

TO SERVE:

warm **chapatti**, **paratha** or **naan**

fresh coriander (optional)

Lots of Indian egg curries contain hard-boiled eggs, but we found that adding the eggs to the pan and poaching them in the curry itself works just as well – if not better, since you get to dip your chapatti in the runny yolk.

If you don't want to open a can of coconut milk to use such a small amount, you can leave it out, but we love the creaminess it gives the curry, and how it well it works with the soft eggs.

Set a medium (approximately 25cm across) frying pan with a lid over a low heat. Add the oil and the onion and cook, stirring until soft and just beginning to brown, about 8 minutes. Add the spices, salt and pepper and cook for 2 minutes, stirring, until really fragrant. Next, add the garlic and green chilli and cook for 1 minute, then tip the tomatoes into the pan. Spread them out into a single layer, add 2 tablespoons of water and cover the pan. Turn the heat up to medium and cook until the tomatoes are collapsing, about 10–15 minutes, stirring occasionally to ensure they don't stick to the bottom of the pan.

When the tomatoes are very saucy, add the frozen spinach, if using. Cook until defrosted and combined into the sauce, then add the coconut milk, if using. Stir to combine.

Turn the heat down to low again. Make 2–4 wells in the the curry mixture (according to the number of eggs you are using) and break an egg into each one. Season each one with salt and a generous grinding of black pepper, cover the pan with a lid and cook for 4–6 minutes (check the eggs every couple of minutes), or until the whites of the eggs are just set.

Serve with warm Indian flatbreads, garnished with fresh coriander, if using.

\\\\ TIP ///

Stretch this meal further by adding chickpeas, or leftover cooked white or sweet potatoes, cut into cubes. Vegans can scramble in some soft tofu instead of using eggs.

PUTTANESCA BAKED EGGS

SERVES 2
PREP TIME: 5 MINS • COOK TIME: 25 MINS
DF (if not buttering your toast)

2 tablespoons **olive oil**

2 cloves of **garlic**, peeled and bruised

5 **anchovies**, salted and packed in oil, drained

¼ teaspoon **chilli flakes**

1 × 400g can of **chopped tomatoes** (it pays to use good-quality canned tomatoes here)

4 **pitted black olives**, roughly diced

2 tablespoons **capers**, drained

2–4 **eggs**, depending on your hunger

TO SERVE:
finely chopped chives
hot toast

For this recipe, we nicked the technique for shakshuka (a Middle Eastern tomato and egg dish which we included in our book **Happy Soups**) *and combined it with Italian puttanesca sauce. We are pretty thrilled with the results. With salty capers, anchovies, chilli, olives and tomato, puttanesca – which is usually made for pasta – is just right with pan-baked eggs. (And hangovers.)*

Set a medium (approximately 25cm across) frying pan with a lid over a low heat. Add the oil and the garlic cloves and let them sizzle for a couple of minutes, infusing their flavour into the oil. Next, add the anchovies and cook, stirring and breaking them up, until they melt into the oil. Add the chilli flakes, then the canned tomatoes. Stir again and cook gently until the tomatoes are soft and saucy, about 15 minutes. Break up any lumps of tomato by pressing with the back of a wooden spoon.

Stir in the olives and capers, then make 2–4 wells in the sauce (according to the number of eggs you are using) and break an egg into each one. Season them each with a little salt and pepper, cover the pan with the lid and cook for 4–6 minutes, or until the whites of the eggs are just set. Discard the garlic, if you can find it, before eating.

Use a wide serving spoon to scoop the eggs and sauce into shallow serving bowls and garnish with chives, if using. Eat with plenty of hot, ideally buttered, toast.

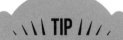

TIP

A handful of fresh parsley or chives is a nice addition to the sauce, but not including them in the recipe makes this the kind of dish you can make after a basic corner-shop dash.

SALMON WITH PUY LENTILS & MUSTARD CRÈME FRAÎCHE

SERVES 2
PREP TIME: 5 MINS · COOK TIME: 15 MINS
WF · GF

2 knobs of **butter**

2 **salmon fillets**

100g long thin stems of **broccoli** (approx. 8 stems)

200g vacuum-packed **ready-cooked Puy lentils**

1–2 teaspoons **smooth Dijon mustard**, to taste

4 tablespoons **crème fraiche**, at room temperature

1 tablespoon **chopped fresh chives**

1 tablespoon **finely chopped fresh parsley**

1–3 teaspoons **lemon juice**, to taste

salt and **freshly ground black pepper**

An old French classic, given a one-pot revamp.

Place a large frying pan over a medium heat and add one of the knobs of butter. Pat dry the salmon fillets and season all over with salt and pepper. When the butter is foaming, tilt the pan to swirl the melted butter over the base. Add the salmon fillets, skin side down, and the broccoli. Cook the fish until the skin is golden brown, about 4 minutes. Turn each fillet and cook until just cooked through, another 3–4 minutes. Turn the broccoli a couple of times as well; it will take on a little colour. When the fish is cooked, remove and set aside; keep warm.

Add the cooked lentils and the second knob of butter along with just enough hot water to loosen them. Bring up to a simmer for a couple of minutes, to warm the lentils through and finish cooking the broccoli, which should retain a good amount of bite.

Meanwhile mix 1 teaspoon of the mustard into the crème fraîche, along with a pinch of salt, then taste and decide if you would like to add more mustard.

Remove the pan from the heat and stir the chives and parsley through the lentils, plus a teaspoon of lemon juice and a little more salt and freshly ground black pepper. Taste and decide if you'd like more lemon juice on the lentils.

Serve the lentils and broccoli with the warm salmon fillets on top, plus a good dollop of the mustard crème fraîche over the fish.

\\\\ TIP ////
Try switching the broccoli for
asparagus or green beans or, for a
dairy-free sauce, serve with salsa
verde instead of crème fraîche.

SMOKY MACKEREL CARBONARA

SERVES 2

PREP TIME: 5 MINS • COOK TIME: 7–10 MINS

200g **spaghetti** or **linguine**

2 **eggs**, beaten

3 tablespoons freshly grated **Parmesan**

2 tablespoons **finely chopped fresh chives**

100g **smoked mackerel**, skin and bones removed, shredded into pieces

1 clove of **garlic**, bruised

freshly ground black pepper

A true carbonara is made with smoked pancetta rather than smoked fish – delicious, but this version is a little healthier because of the valuable fats in mackerel. Be sure to let the egg sauce cook in the residual heat of the pan and hot pasta, rather than on the hob – it should be beautifully creamy, but if it gets too hot it will scramble.

Place the pasta in a large deep pan of boiling, salted water. Cook for about 7 minutes, or until al dente. Meanwhile whisk together the eggs, Parmesan, chives and black pepper.

Scoop out about 50ml of pasta cooking water, then drain the pasta. Return it to the hot pan, off the heat, with the mackerel, the egg mixture and the garlic. Stir, still off the heat, tossing it over and over again, for a couple of minutes, until the mackerel is warmed through and the egg has created a smooth sauce. If it seems at all dry or sticky, gradually add some of the warm reserved pasta water. (You almost certainly won't need any salt because of the fish and cheese.)

Remove the garlic and serve immediately.

\\\\ TIP ////

If you'd rather make a traditional porky carbonara, leave out the chives, and fry 100g of smoked pancetta in the pan you're going to cook the pasta in, reserve it and add it at the end with the eggs.

SEARED BEEF & GREENS STIR-FRY

SERVES 2

PREP TIME: 15 MINS • COOK TIME: 15 MINS

(WF • GF if using rice noodles and check soy sauce ingredients) • DF

1 head of **pak choy** (about 200g)

150g **long-stemmed broccoli**
(ideally **tenderstem** or **purple
sprouting**)

150g **long green beans (fine, French**
or **round)**

3 tablespoons **vegetable oil**

250g **rump steak**, fat trimmed, at
room temperature

250g **ready-cooked rice noodles** or
wheat noodles

a large handful of **bean sprouts**

SAUCE:

3cm piece of **fresh ginger**, peeled
and grated

1 clove of **garlic**, grated

3 teaspoons **fresh red chilli**, seeded and
finely chopped

3 tablespoons **soy sauce**

2 tablespoons **fish sauce**

TO SERVE:

4 tablespoons chopped roasted **peanuts**

a small handful of **fresh Thai** or
Italian basil leaves, torn

a small handful of **fresh
coriander leaves**

4 sprigs of **fresh mint**, leaves only

1 **spring onion**, trimmed, halved
lengthwise and sliced on an angle

*Rather than adding the aromatics to the pan and cooking them, use
them like a dressing and add them after the main ingredients are
cooked. This keeps their flavours rich, punchy and fresh. Don't hold
back on the mint – it works brilliantly with rare beef.*

Wash and prepare all the vegetables before you start cooking: trim the pak choy,
removing the base of the bulb, and chop into bite-sized pieces. Break the broccoli
into small florets and trim any woody pieces from the stems. Trim the beans.

Whisk together the ginger, garlic, chilli, soy sauce and fish sauce. Set aside.

Set a wok over a high heat and add a tablespoon of the vegetable oil. Pat the steak
dry with kitchen paper. When the pan is smoking hot, add the beef. Cook until rare
(or more if you prefer), about 3 minutes a side for a 2½cm thick steak. Remove from
the pan and set aside to rest while you prepare the rest of the stir-fry.

Carefully wipe most of the oil and beef fat out of the wok, using kitchen paper.
Pour in 2 tablespoons of fresh vegetable oil. When very hot, add the broccoli and
green beans and cook, stirring, for 2 minutes. Next add the pak choy and cook,
stirring, for 2 minutes. (The vegetables should be barely cooked, with plenty of
crunch.) Add the cooked noodles and the bean sprouts and cook, again stirring all
the time, for 2 minutes, or until the noodles are heated through. Remove the pan
from the heat. Going against the grain, slice the beef into ½cm thick strips. Add
to the pan along with the sauce and stir thoroughly to coat.

Divide the stir-fry between 2 bowls, topping each with half the peanuts, basil,
coriander, mint and spring onion. Eat immediately.

\\\\ TIP ////

The key to any stir-fry is having absolutely everything lined up and ready to go before you start cooking – a mushy, wet stir-fry makes a pretty sad supper.

KEDGEREE HASH

SERVES 2
PREP TIME: 10 MINS • COOK TIME: 20 MINS
WF · GF · DF

400g **Maris Piper potatoes**,
   washed and coarsely grated
3 tablespoons **olive oil**
½ **onion**, coarsely grated
250g **undyed, skinless, boneless
   smoked haddock**, chopped into 2cm
   pieces (check for rogue bones
   as you chop)
2 tablespoons **chopped fresh chives**
1 teaspoon **curry powder**,
   or more to taste
2–4 **eggs**, depending on your hunger
salt and **freshly ground black pepper**
a handful of **fresh coriander**, to serve

Inspired by the classic kedgeree pairing of smoked fish, egg and curry spices, this is warming and hearty.

Tip the grated potatoes on to a clean tea towel. Wrap them up and squeeze out their liquid over the sink.

Use a large wide frying pan with a lid. Set it over a low–medium heat, and add the oil. When hot (but not smoking), add the potatoes, grated onion and a tiny pinch of salt – both the fish and curry powder may be salty so you don't need much, but adding it here it will stop the onion and potato browning too fast. Spread everything out evenly, then cover and cook gently for 8 minutes, stirring and spreading out again every minute or two. The potato will turn golden brown in places. Add the chopped fish and stir to combine, then cover and cook for 2 minutes, until the fish is just cooked.

Add the chives, some black pepper and the curry powder and stir gently to mix. Taste and correct the seasoning, or add more curry powder, if you like. Make 2–4 wells in the mixture, depending on the number of eggs you are using, and break an egg into each one. Cover the pan again and cook for around 4–6 minutes, or until the whites of the eggs are just set. Serve each portion with a little fresh coriander on top.

\\\ TIP ///

If kedgeree isn't your thing, leave out the curry powder and mimic the flavour of smoked haddock chowder by adding a handful of frozen sweetcorn along with the fish, and, instead of coriander, serve with chopped fresh parsley.
Or, for a chunkier texture, sauté cubed potatoes until cooked through and golden, rather than grating them.

FRESH & EASY

FENNEL & ORANGE BAKED FISH

SERVES 4
PREP TIME: 15 MINS • COOK TIME: 40 MINS
WF · GF · DF

1 **orange** (ideally organic and unwaxed), zested and thinly sliced

1 small **white onion**, thinly sliced

2 heads of **fennel** (about 600g, outer layers discarded if tough), thinly sliced

2 medium **potatoes** (about 500g), thinly sliced

½ teaspoon **fennel seeds**

2 cloves of **garlic**, minced

3 tablespoons **olive oil**

4 **salmon fillets**

2 tablespoons **finely chopped fresh parsley**

salt and **freshly ground black pepper**

A summery delish fish dish. Make sure you cut the vegetables and orange slices to the same thickness to ensure even cooking.

Heat the oven to 180°C/350°F/gas mark 4.

Place the vegetables and orange slices in a large roasting dish. Add the fennel seeds, garlic, a pinch of salt, 1 teaspoon of freshly ground black pepper and the olive oil. Mix well and evenly distribute everything across the dish. Bake in the preheated oven for 30 minutes, turning everything once halfway through. Check that the potatoes are tender and the fennel is soft before adding the salmon – if not, return the dish to the oven for 5–10 minutes.

Coat the salmon with the orange zest, more black pepper and a little salt, then place on top of the fennel mix and put the dish back into the oven for 8–10 minutes, or until the fish is just cooked.

Top with the parsley to serve.

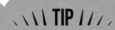

TIP
This also works with whole trout. Tuck the orange zest into the cavity and increase the cooking time for the fish to about 20 minutes.

4
NO-COOK
PASTA
SAUCES

SICILIAN-STYLE PESTO ALLA TRAPANESE

SERVES 4
PREP TIME: 10 MINS • COOK TIME: 8 MINS
DF · V · Ve (if Parmesan omitted)

450g **dried twisty pasta**, ideally
Sicilian **busiati**, but if not available
use **fusilli**, **spirali** or **gemilli**

1 large clove of **garlic** (blanched for
3 minutes in a cup of boiling water for
a milder taste)

50g **blanched almonds**, chopped

3 large handfuls **fresh basil**, leaves only

3–4 tablespoons good-quality
extra virgin olive oil

400g very ripe **tomatoes**, seeded
and finely chopped

salt and **freshly ground black pepper**

freshly grated Parmesan,
to serve (optional)

Traditionally, almond and tomato pesto alla Trapanese, from Sicily, is made in a pestle and mortar. You can make this in a blender or food processor without much impact on its taste, but the high-speed blades will mean you end up with a brownish sauce, rather than a pleasingly green and red-flecked one.

Place the pasta in a large pan of boiling salted water and cook for about 8 minutes, or until al dente.

Meanwhile make the sauce: use a pestle to pound the garlic with a generous pinch of salt in a mixing bowl until it forms a paste, then add the almonds and grind them until like gritty sand. Add the basil and continue to pound. Add the oil and mix, then add the tomatoes and pound again until the whole thing resembles a chunky but creamy sauce.

Drain the cooked pasta, reserving a couple of tablespoons of cooking water. Return the pasta to the hot pan and add the pesto, a dusting of freshly ground black pepper and reserved cooking water. Toss very thoroughly, then taste – you may feel it needs a bit more salt and another teaspoon or tablespoon of oil. Toss again, then serve with fresh Parmesan, if using.

TIP

To make this dairy free, instead of
Parmesan, serve it with a sprinkling
of crunchy toasted breadcrumbs or
pangrattato (see our previous book,
Happy Soups, for a recipe).

CAULIFLOWER & CAPER

SERVES 4
PREP TIME: 15 MINS • COOK TIME: 8 MINS
V (if vegetarian Parmesan is used)

400g **dried bucatini** (or **spaghetti** or **linguine**)

zest of ½–1 small **unwaxed lemon**, finely grated

300g **cauliflower florets**

12 **walnut halves**

3 tablespoons **roughly chopped fresh parsley**

2 tablespoons **capers**, drained

20g **freshly grated Parmesan**, plus more to serve

1 clove of **garlic** (blanched for 3 minutes in a cup of boiling water for a milder taste)

3 tablespoons good-quality **extra virgin olive oil**

½ teaspoon **sherry vinegar** or **red wine vinegar**

salt

We admit, a raw cauliflower sauce for pasta sounds mad. But we discovered this technique via the New York-based food writer Deb Perelman, aka Smitten Kitchen, and we can't get enough. This is a spin on her recipe, but is also influenced by a roast cauliflower pasta cooked by chef Mario Batali. You could follow Batali's lead and roast the cauliflower florets for 10 minutes in a hot oven before blitzing them in the sauce.

Place the pasta in a large pan of boiling salted water and cook for about 8 minutes, or until al dente.

Meanwhile, put the zest of half the lemon, a generous pinch of salt and all the other ingredients, apart from the oil and vinegar, into the bowl of a food processor and blitz until the cauliflower looks like quinoa or couscous. Remove the blade and stir in the oil and vinegar.

When the pasta is cooked, remove from the heat, reserve 3 tablespoons of the cooking water, and drain. Return the pasta to the hot pan and add the cauliflower mixture and the reserved water. Toss really thoroughly, then taste and add more salt and the rest of lemon zest, as necessary.

Serve with freshly grated Parmesan.

\\\ TIP ///
This dish works well with a pinch of dried chilli added. Omit the oil and use the blitzed cauliflower mixture as the base for a salad, in place of bulgur wheat or couscous.

ROASTED PEPPER
& ANCHOVY

SERVES 4
PREP TIME: 5 MINS · COOK TIME: 8 MINS
DF

450g **dried linguine**

4 tablespoons **roasted pepper paste**, from a jar

8 **anchovies**, salted and packed in oil, drained

1 teaspoon **dried chilli flakes**, or to taste

1 large clove of **garlic** (blanched for 3 minutes in a cup of boiling water for a milder taste)

2 tablespoons **blanched almonds**

3 tablespoons good-quality **extra virgin olive oil**

½ teaspoon **fennel seeds** (optional)

Anchovies, chillies and almonds give this no-cook pasta sauce a huge umami hit.

Place the pasta in a large pan of boiling salted water and cook for about 8 minutes, or until al dente.

Meanwhile make the sauce. You can either blitz it in a food processor, or pulverize it in a pestle and mortar – we prefer the more rugged texture you get in a mortar; if you use a food processor, be sure to stop when the sauce is a rough paste, rather than completely smooth.

Either way, mix together the pepper paste, anchovies, chilli flakes, garlic, almonds and oil, then process until you reach a pesto-like consistency. If using, add the fennel seeds right at the end and process or pummel very briefly – you just want to bruise them, otherwise their flavour will be too powerful.

Taste the sauce – because of the anchovies, you almost certainly won't need any more salt, but you could add more chilli.

Drain the pasta, saving a couple of tablespoons of the cooking water. Return it to the hot pan along with the sauce and the reserved cooking water and toss very thoroughly, until the sauce coats the pasta. Serve straight away.

TIP

Vegetarians and vegans can omit the anchovies but will need to add a good pinch of salt to the sauce instead.

SUGO DI POMODORO CRUDO

SERVES 4

PREP TIME: 5 MINS, plus 3–4 hours standing • COOK TIME: 7 MINS

DF • V • Ve

500g very ripe **tomatoes**, seeded and very finely diced

4 tablespoons good-quality **extra virgin olive oil**

2 cloves of **garlic**, crushed to a paste

1½ teaspoons **sherry vinegar** or **red wine vinegar**

a generous handful of **fresh basil**, leaves only, roughly torn

flaky sea salt

400g **dried spaghetti**

This Italian sauce is completely delicious and absurdly simple to make.

Three or four hours before you want to eat, mix together the tomatoes, oil, garlic, vinegar, basil and a generous pinch of salt. Cover and leave at room temperature for the flavours to develop.

When ready to eat, cook the pasta in boiling salted water for a minute less than the packet instructions, until al dente. Drain, then return to the hot pan, off the heat. Tip the tomato mixture into the pan and stir vigorously, so that the starch from the pasta melds with the oil and tomato juices and coats the pasta. Serve straight away.

TIP

This vegan dish is wonderful without cheese, but do also try it with some goats' cheese, Parmesan, ricotta salata or buffalo mozzarella (all at room temperature). Alternatively make it with chopped capers instead of vinegar.

SINGAPORE NOODLES

SERVES 4

PREP TIME: 15 MINS, plus noodle soaking • COOK TIME: 8 MINS

WF • GF (check soy sauce ingredients) • DF

. . . .

200g **dried rice vermicelli/rice stick noodles**

100g **long green beans (fine, French or round)**

a handful of **cabbage**, finely shredded

2 **spring onions**, sliced on an angle into 1cm pieces

1 **green pepper**, seeded and sliced into strips

100g **bean sprouts**

1 tablespoon **soy sauce**

2 teaspoons **fish sauce**

5 tablespoons **dry white wine, dry sherry** or **rice wine**

a generous pinch of **sugar**

2 teaspoons **Madras curry powder**

½ teaspoon **ground turmeric**

5cm piece of **fresh ginger**, peeled and finely grated

2 cloves of **garlic**, finely grated

3 teaspoons **fresh red chilli**, seeded and finely chopped

2 **eggs**

2 tablespoons **vegetable** or **sesame oil**

400g **raw shelled prawns**

salt and **freshly ground black pepper**

TO SERVE:
fresh coriander leaves
soy sauce

Oddly, you'll never find this stir-fried curry noodle dish in Singapore itself. Just like we don't really eat English muffins in England.

Rice stick or rice vermicelli noodles are available in large supermarkets, in Asian food stores and online.

. . . .

Soak the noodles in boiling water according to the packet instructions, then drain and set aside.

Prepare the vegetables so they are all ready to go into the wok.

Whisk together the soy sauce, fish sauce, wine, sugar, curry powder, turmeric, ginger, garlic, chilli and a pinch of salt. Set aside.

Break the eggs into a bowl and beat well, adding 1 teaspoon of the soy sauce mixture and a little salt and pepper. Set aside.

When everything is ready, pour the oil into a large wok set over a high heat. When very hot, add the vegetables and the remaining sauce mixture and stir-fry for 2 minutes. Next add the raw prawns and drained noodles and cook, stirring again, until the prawns are cooked through and the noodles are tender. Push the stir-fry to the side of the pan and add the eggs. Cook for just a minute or so, until barely set, gently scraping the cooked eggs away from the sides as you would an omelette. When almost cooked, break up the eggs and mix into the stir-fry.

Serve immediately in wide bowls, with a handful of fresh coriander leaves on each portion and extra soy sauce on the side.

\ \ \ \ TIP / / / /

Add cooked char siu pork, leftover roast pork or cooked, shredded chicken. American versions of the recipe often include strips of red pepper and add a handful of peas.

THAI BAKED BREAM

SERVES 4

PREP TIME: 10 MINS • COOK TIME: 25 MINS

WF • GF • DF

2 **whole sea bream**, cleaned and gutted

400ml **full-fat coconut milk**
 from a well-shaken can

1 stick of **lemongrass**, cut into 3 and
 roughly bruised

zest of ¼ **lime**

3 **lime leaves**, roughly torn

½ teaspoon **ground turmeric**

a pinch of **hot chilli powder**,
 or more, to taste

3cm piece of **fresh ginger**, peeled
 and grated

2 cloves of **garlic**, peeled and
 roughly bruised

1 tablespoon **fish sauce**

400g **long green beans (fine**
 or French)

salt and **freshly ground black pepper**

a handful of **roughly chopped**
 fresh coriander or **Thai basil**, to serve

The fish are half poached, half roasted in a delicately spiced coconut curry. This technique is incredibly simple: just chuck everything into a baking dish and bake.

Heat the oven to 200°C/400°F/gas mark 6.

Choose a baking dish into which both the fish will fit fairly snugly, so that the bottom of the fish poaches in the aromatic coconut milk and the liquid doesn't dry out.

Pour the coconut milk into the dish and add the lemongrass, lime zest, lime leaves, turmeric, chilli powder, ginger, garlic and fish sauce. Mix thoroughly.

Pat the outside of the fish dry using kitchen paper, then cut three deep diagonal slashes across the top of each fish, to allow the flavours to penetrate. Season the fish all over with salt and pepper. Lay the fish on top of the coconut mixture, spooning some over the top, and place in the preheated oven.

Bake for 10 minutes, then remove from the oven, baste with the coconut mixture, and tuck the beans into the coconut too. Return to the oven for a further 15 minutes.

Check the fish is cooked through: it should flake easily away from the bone. To serve, lift each whole fish out of the cooking liquor and cut portions of it away from the bone. Use a slotted spoon to remove each serving of beans from the coconut curry (leave the lime leaf, garlic cloves and lemongrass behind), then serve the fish on top of the beans. Pour over some of the curry and finish with a handful of coriander or Thai basil. Serve straight away.

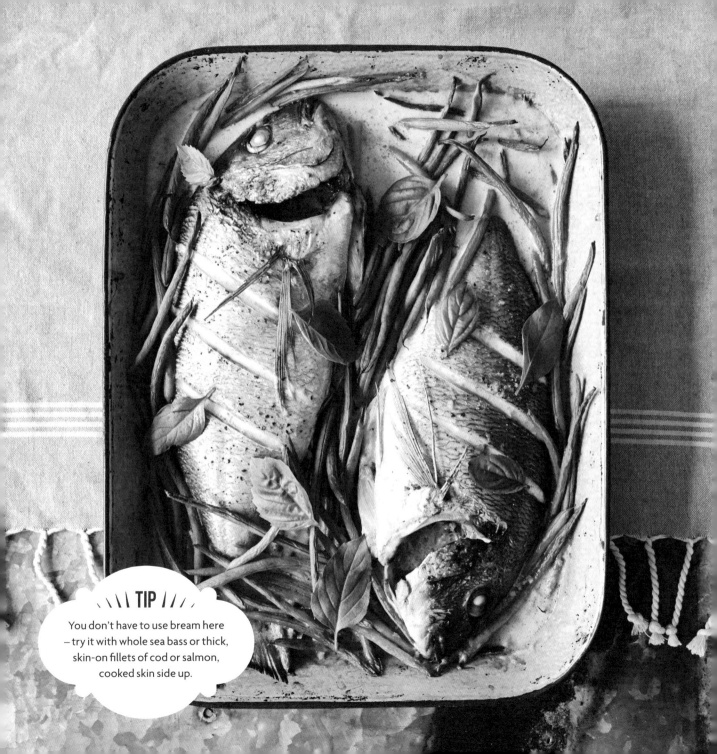

BUDDHA'S DELIGHT

SERVES 4 (pictured overleaf)

PREP TIME: 15 MINS, plus 2 hours soaking · COOK TIME: 10 MINS

WF · GF (check soy sauce ingredients) · DF · V · Ve

This vegan Chinese dish is often cooked on New Year's day, and sits – deliciously – halfway between a stir-fry and a vegetable braise.

Getting all the ingredients together will probably mean a trip to an Asian supermarket or website, but the end result makes the effort absolutely worthwhile. Dried bean curd sticks are a kind of tofu and need soaking before use – they have a delicate, creamy flavour. Preserved fermented red bean curd lends an intense umami burst to everything it is used in. Cooked bamboo shoots come in cans or vacuum packs, and both glass noodles and Shaoxing rice wine are often available in larger supermarkets.

15 **dried shiitake mushrooms**

100g **dried bean curd sticks**

100g **dried mung bean/
   glass noodles**

2 tablespoons **flavourless oil**

1 × 4cm piece of **fresh ginger**, peeled
   and finely sliced

3 cloves of **garlic**, finely sliced

3 heaped tablespoons **preserved red
   bean curd** (hot or mild)

125g **carrots**, sliced into thin strips

5 **spring onions**, sliced on an angle into
   2cm pieces + **1 spring onion**, finely
   chopped, to serve

½ head of **Chinese (napa) cabbage**,
   thickly sliced

150g **mangetout**

100g **ready-cooked bamboo shoots**,
   roughly chopped

salt

25g roasted **unsalted
   peanuts**, chopped, to serve

SAUCE:

2 tablespoons **soy sauce**

2 tablespoons **Shaoxing Chinese rice
   wine** or **dry sherry**

3 tablespoons **mushroom soaking liquid**
   (see recipe)

½ teaspoon **maple syrup**

Two hours before you want to cook, separately cover the dried shiitake mushrooms and bean curd sticks with boiling water and leave to rehydrate. Ten minutes before you want to cook, cover the noodles with boiling water and leave to rehydrate for 10 minutes (or soak according to the packet instructions – some require longer). Drain and set aside.

Drain the bean curd sticks thoroughly and slice each stick in half. Drain and squeeze out the mushrooms, keeping the soaking liquid, then slice into small pieces.

Make the sauce by whisking all the ingredients together. As with any stir-fry, prepare all the other ingredients before you start cooking.

Place a large wok over a low–medium heat. Add the oil, ginger, garlic and mushrooms and stir-fry for 2 minutes. Add the preserved red bean curd and mash until smooth in the pan. Add the drained bean curd sticks and stir to coat, then add the carrots and spring onions (reserving the finely chopped spring onion to garnish). Cook for 5 minutes, stirring gently and often. Next, add the cabbage, mangetout and bamboo shoots and cook for 2 minutes. Finally add a good pinch of salt, the sauce and the drained noodles and toss, still on the heat, very thoroughly to coat everything in the sauce. Let the sauce cook for about a minute.

Divide between 4 warmed bowls and top with the chopped peanuts and reserved finely chopped spring onion.

\\\\ TIP ////

There is no set recipe for Buddha's delight – it varies from family to family, so if you can't get some of the ingredients, don't worry. You could just as easily use fresh mushrooms or normal extra-firm tofu; feel free to add seasonal vegetables like green beans or broccoli.

BUDDHA'S
DELIGHT

CRAB LINGUINE WITH CHILLI & LEMON

SERVES 4
PREP TIME: 10 MINS • COOK TIME: 10 MINS
DF

. . . .

400g **dried linguine**

200g **prepared white crab meat**

2–4 teaspoons finely chopped **fresh red chilli**, to taste

1 clove of **garlic**, bruised

3–5 tablespoons **extra virgin olive oil**, to taste

1–2 tablespoons **freshly squeezed lemon juice**, to taste

1½ tablespoons **finely chopped fresh parsley**

flaky sea salt and **freshly ground black pepper**

John would like to dedicate this to Katie, in remembrance of noughties holidays.

. . . .

Place a deep saucepan filled with boiling, salted water over a medium heat and bring back to the boil. Add the linguine and cook for a minute less than the packet suggests.

Drain, but not too thoroughly, and return to the pan slightly wet. Stir in the crab meat, chopped chilli, bruised garlic, 3 tablespoons of extra virgin olive oil, 1 tablespoon of lemon juice, a good pinch of sea salt, some black pepper and the parsley. Stir thoroughly and taste, then decide if you would like more oil, lemon or salt.

Remove the garlic, then serve straight away.

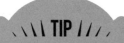

\\\ TIP ///
This is popular with small children – use sweet red pepper in place of the chilli.

SPRING VEGETABLE STIR-FRY

SERVES 4
PREP TIME: 20 MINS • COOK TIME: 15 MINS
(WF • GF if using rice noodles but check soy sauce ingredients) • DF • V • Ve

SAUCE:

¼ teaspoon **hot chilli powder**

3 tablespoons **soy sauce**

1 tablespoon **freshly squeezed lime juice**

1 × 2cm piece of **fresh ginger**, peeled and grated

1 clove of **garlic**, crushed

STIR-FRY:

300g **firm tofu**, cut into 2cm cubes

1 tablespoon **maple syrup**

½ teaspoon **hot chilli powder**

5 tablespoons **flavourless cooking oil**

1 large **aubergine**, cut into 2cm cubes

75g **mangetout**

250g **pak choy**, trimmed and cut into bite-sized pieces

100g **broccoli** (ideally long-stemmed), cut into florets

100g **long green beans** (fine, **round** or **French**)

300g **ready-cooked wheat** or **rice noodles**, thin or fine

3 **spring onions**, finely diced

a handful of **fresh coriander leaves**

A crunchy, punchy spring stir-fry.

Whisk the sauce ingredients together and set aside.

Place the tofu on a couple of sheets of kitchen paper; top with another sheet and press gently to absorb excess water. Mix the maple syrup and chilli powder together and toss the tofu in the mixture.

Place a large wok over a high heat and pour in the oil. When shimmering hot, add the tofu and fry until golden on the bottom of each piece – it will initially stick to the wok, then release when cooked, so try to wait before turning it. When golden, lift out the tofu, letting the excess oil drain back into the pan, and set aside, then add the aubergine to the hot oil. Fry for 4–5 minutes, until golden. Next, add the mangetout, pak choy, broccoli and green beans. Cook for 2 minutes, then add the noodles and the cooked tofu and cook for another 2 minutes. Remove from the heat, add the sauce, spring onions and coriander leaves and toss to coat.

Serve straight away, in wide bowls.

TIP

Like all stir-fries, you can customize this one — add crushed toasted peanuts, egg, cooked seafood or use ready-seasoned tofu instead of plain.

SARDINES WITH TOMATOES, ROSEMARY & WHITE BEANS

SERVES 4

PREP TIME: 12 MINS • COOK TIME: 22 MINS

(WF · GF if served without bread) · DF

400g **cherry tomatoes**, halved

4 tablespoons **olive oil**

3 sprigs of **fresh rosemary**

4 cloves of **garlic**, peeled and bruised

12 **whole fresh sardines**, cleaned, gutted and loose scales removed by your fishmonger

1 × 400g can of **cannellini beans**, drained and rinsed

salt and **freshly ground black pepper**

crusty bread, to serve

Sardines are oily fish and stuffed with omega-3 fatty acids, something almost all of us should eat more of. These good fats and rosemary are both a key part of the Mediterranean diet – check out the Italian village of Acciaroli, where there are many centenarians and where they eat a lot of rosemary. (Alternatively, drink some rosemary water.) There's nothing worthy about this punchy, flavourful Mediterranean-inspired dish, though.

Heat the oven to 180°C/350°F/gas mark 4.

Tip the halved tomatoes into a baking dish, along with 3 tablespoons of the oil, the rosemary, garlic and some salt and pepper. Place in the preheated oven for 15 minutes, checking just before the end of cooking.

Meanwhile season the sardines with more salt and pepper and brush with the remaining oil. Remove the dish of tomatoes from the oven and stir in the beans. Arrange the sardines on top and return to the oven for 7 minutes, or until the fish is just beginning to flake away from the bone.

Serve with crusty bread to mop up the pan juices.

\\\ TIP ///

If you don't fancy sardines, try this with fillets of mackerel, cooked skin side up.

AVOCADO PESTO PASTA

SERVES 4
PREP TIME: 8 MINS · COOK TIME: 8 MINS
DF · (V · Ve if Parmesan omitted)

450g **dried linguine**

2 **ripe avocados**

1 large clove of **garlic**, blanched for 3 minutes in a cup of boiling water, then crushed

3 tablespoons **pine nuts**

3 tablespoons good-quality **extra virgin olive oil**

3 large handfuls **fresh basil**, leaves only

3 tablespoons **freshly grated Parmesan** (optional – vegans can leave it out and vegetarians can use a vegetarian brand)

2 teaspoons **lemon juice**

flaky sea salt

This idea was a hot tip from Rebecca's friend Kate, who uses it to get more green vegetables into her toddlers, while also making a meal adults will like. The creamy, bright green pesto is very family-friendly, and you can easily involve small people in making it.

Place the pasta in a large pan of boiling salted water and cook for about 8 minutes, or until al dente.

Meanwhile make the sauce. You can either blitz it in a food processor, or pulverize it in a pestle and mortar – we prefer the more rugged texture you get in a mortar; if you use a food processor, be sure to stop when the sauce is a rough paste, rather than completely smooth.

Either way, mix together the avocado flesh, garlic, pine nuts, oil and a generous pinch of salt and process briefly. Next add the basil leaves and the Parmesan, if using, and process to form a rough paste. Taste and very gradually add the lemon juice – the aim is not to make the sauce lemony, instead the acidity just brightens the flavour of the pesto.

Drain the cooked pasta, saving a couple of tablespoons of the cooking water. Return the pasta to the hot pan along with the sauce and the reserved cooking water and toss very thoroughly. Serve straight away.

\\\ TIP ///
Avocado and chilli are a match made in heaven, so if you're not making this for kids, add some hot or mild chilli flakes when serving.

BAKED FISH CURRY

SERVES 4

PREP TIME: 15 MINS • COOK TIME: 15 MINS

(WF • GF if served with rice) • DF

1 tablespoon **flavourless cooking oil**

1 large **onion**, finely grated

2 clove of **fresh garlic**, crushed

1 × 5cm piece of **fresh ginger**, peeled and finely grated

1 teaspoon **ground cumin**

1 teaspoon **mustard seeds**

1 teaspoon **ground turmeric**

1 **hot green chilli**, seeded and finely chopped

1½ teaspoons **tamarind paste**

8 **curry leaves**

¼–½ teaspoon **cayenne**, to taste

600ml **full-fat coconut milk** from well-shaken cans

500g **skinless, boneless fish fillets**, cut into chunks (**cod**, **hake**, **haddock**, **salmon** or **trout** all work well, or try a mixture)

salt and **freshly ground black pepper**

TO SERVE:

fresh coriander leaves

Indian flatbreads or **microwave rice**

After briefly toasting the onions and spices on the hob, this tray-baked fragrant South Indian style curry is finished in the oven. John was taught this dish on a trip to Kerala way back in 2005.

Sour-but-sweet tamarind paste or concentrate is widely available in supermarkets. Avoid low-fat coconut milk, as it's more likely to split when heated.

Heat the oven to 200°C/400°F/gas mark 6.

Use an ovenproof metal pan for this curry. Set it over a medium heat and add the oil. When hot, add the grated onion and let sizzle for a minute or two, then add the garlic, ginger and dried spices. Cook, stirring, for a couple of minutes, until really fragrant.

Now add everything except the fish. Add a big pinch of salt and some black pepper and stir really well to combine. Add the fish chunks, spreading them out in a single layer and spooning the sauce over each piece. Place in the preheated oven for 10 minutes, or until the fish is just cooked through.

Serve straight away, scattered with coriander leaves and with flatbreads or rice alongside.

\\\ **TIP** ///

Vegetarians can skip the
fish and replace it with
cubes of aubergine,
sautéd with the onion,
long green beans,
or leftover cooked
vegetables like butternut
squash and sweet potato.

WINTER STIR-FRY

SERVES 2–3

PREP TIME: 20 MINS • COOK TIME: 10 MINS

WF • GF (check soy sauce ingredients) • DF • V

. . . .

SAUCE:

2 tablespoons **sriracha hot sauce**

2 tablespoons **soy sauce**

1½ tablespoons **freshly squeezed lime juice**

1 × 3cm piece of **fresh ginger**, peeled and grated

1 small clove of **garlic**, grated (blanch in a cup of boiling water for 3 minutes for a milder taste) (optional)

STIR-FRY:

3 tablespoons **flavourless oil**

3 **eggs**, beaten

a splash of **soy sauce**

100g **Brussels sprouts**, trimmed and quartered

4 **shiitake mushrooms**, torn into bite-sized pieces (or use any kind of small **mushroom**)

100g **cauliflower**, broken into small florets

100g **kale**, ribs removed, shredded

200g **ready-cooked thick udon-style noodles**

TO SERVE:

1 **spring onion**, finely chopped

fresh coriander

A health-giving stir-fry to perk up winter days.

Sriracha is a bright red Thai hot sauce, and is easy to find in Asian food stores and large supermarkets.

. . . .

Whisk together the sauce ingredients.

Prepare all the stir-fry ingredients before you start to cook, as everything should be added in quick succession.

Pour 1 tablespoon of the oil into a large wok. When hot, add the eggs and soy sauce and scramble very briefly, for just a minute, then scoop them out and set to one side (use the bowl they were beaten in, as they will be cooked again at the end).

Add the rest of the oil to the wok and, when hot, tip in the sprouts, mushrooms and cauliflower. Stir-fry for about 3 minutes, until the cauliflower and sprouts take on a little colour. Next, add the kale and stir-fry for a further 2 minutes. Add the noodles and the scrambled egg and stir-fry for 1 minute. Remove from the heat and pour over the sauce. Toss well, then divide between serving bowls. Scatter over the spring onion and coriander, and eat straight away.

\\\ TIP ///

A handful of bashed-up roasted peanuts adds protein and crunch, especially for vegans, who can omit the eggs.

POSH

BEEF BOURGUIGNON WITH POTATOES

SERVES 4

PREP TIME: 25 MINS • COOK TIME: 3 HOURS

(WF • GF if served without bread) • DF

3 tablespoons **flavourless oil**

75g **unsmoked streaky bacon**
  or **pancetta**, diced

200g **small round mushrooms**
  (**chestnut**, **button** or **closed cup**),
  chopped into bite-sized pieces
  if necessary

150g **carrots**, cut into thin half-moons

200g **pearl onions** or **shallots**,
  halved if large

500g **beef shin**, cut into chunks

500ml **Pinot Noir red wine** (or something
  soft and smooth, not cheap plonk)

250ml hot **beef stock**

2 **bay leaves**

2 sprigs of **fresh parsley**

2 sprigs of **fresh thyme**

2 cloves of **garlic**

400g **new potatoes**, halved

3 tablespoons **roughly chopped
  fresh parsley**

salt and **freshly ground black pepper**

crusty bread, to serve (optional)

Beef bourguignon is a classic French stew from Burgundy, one to leave simmering away on a chilly weekend afternoon. We've simplified the recipe slightly and, to make it a true one-pot, we cook the potatoes in the rich, dark beefy sauce.

Cheap, sharp wine or wine with lots of tannins won't work well for this – purists insist on something from Burgundy, but as that can be pricey, just choose a mellow, drinkable red.

Set a large casserole dish with a lid over a high heat. Add 1 tablespoon of oil and, when hot, add the bacon or pancetta. Fry until crisp, then lift out and reserve in a bowl, leaving any fat behind. Add the mushrooms to the pan and sauté until golden, about 5 minutes. Lift out and place with the bacon. Add another spoonful of oil, if needed. Tip the carrots and pearl onions or shallots into the pan and sauté for 6–8 minutes, until the onions begin to caramelize. Again, lift out and reserve with the bacon and mushrooms.

Next add the beef shin and another spoonful of oil if the pan looks dry. Brown the beef thoroughly, then add the red wine and hot stock. If you can, make a bouquet garni by tying the bay leaves, parsley sprigs, thyme and garlic up in a little square of muslin. If not, pop them all into the pan loose, but remember to fish them out before serving. Season with a little salt and lots of black pepper.

Bring the liquid up to a simmer, cover with the lid and cook for 1½ hours. Add the reserved bacon, mushrooms, carrots and onions and simmer for another 30 minutes. Check that the beef is meltingly tender, and if so, add the new potatoes. Simmer for a further 30 minutes without the lid.

Taste before serving to check that the potatoes are done and add more salt and pepper, as necessary. Sprinkle the fresh parsley over the stew before serving in wide shallow bowls, perhaps with a little crusty bread to mop up the sauce.

\\\\ TIP ////

If you can find sweet
baby carrots, leave them whole
and cook them as they are.

CHICKEN WITH ARTICHOKES, LEEKS & TARRAGON

SERVES 2

PREP TIME: 5 MINS • COOK TIME: 15 MINS

1 tablespoon **olive oil**

2 skinless, boneless **chicken breasts**, cut into bite-sized pieces

1 **leek**, finely sliced

300ml hot, good-quality **chicken stock**

250g **fresh egg tagliatelle**

150g **cooked artichoke hearts** from a jar or can, cut into bite-sized pieces

2 teaspoons **freshly squeezed lemon juice**

zest of ½ **lemon**

3 tablespoons **freshly grated Parmesan**, plus more to serve

1–2 tablespoons **double cream** (optional)

2 tablespoons **roughly chopped fresh tarragon leaves**

freshly ground black pepper

The cream is not essential if you want to make this a lighter meal.

Pour the oil into a wide high-sided pan with a lid, set over a low heat. Season the meat all over. Place the chicken and the leek in the pan and cook, stirring often, until the chicken is just beginning to brown and the leek is soft. Remove from the pan and set aside – the chicken probably won't be fully cooked, but don't worry as it should cook through in the next step.

Pour the hot stock into the same pan, bring to the boil, then add the pasta. Place the chicken and leeks on top of the pasta, weighing it down into the liquid. Cover with the lid and cook for 4 minutes (or according to the pasta packet instructions).

Remove from the heat. Check that the chicken is cooked through, then stir in the artichoke hearts (they will warm through in the sauce), lots of black pepper, the lemon juice, lemon zest and Parmesan. Add the cream, if using, and the tarragon. Toss several times to help the sauce emulsify. Taste and decide you would like more black pepper or cheese, and serve straight away.

COQ AU VIN IN THE OVEN

SERVES 4

PREP TIME: 15 MINS • COOK TIME: 1 HOUR 40 MINS

DF

8 **shallots**, halved

1 **onion**, sliced into 8 wedges

125g **chestnut** or **button mushrooms**,
 halved if large

1 large **carrot**, finely diced

1 stick of **celery**, finely diced

2 tablespoons **olive oil**

4 whole **chicken legs**, or a mixture of
 chicken thighs and **drumsticks**

50g **smoked back bacon**,
 cut into small pieces

500ml **red wine** (choose something
 smooth and mellow, not spicy or full
 of harsh tannins)

2 cloves of **garlic**, crushed

3 sprigs of **fresh thyme**

1 **bay leaf**

200ml hot **chicken stock**

3 tablespoons **plain flour**

salt and **freshly ground black pepper**

TO SERVE:

finely chopped fresh parsley

crusty bread

Usually coq au vin involves several stages of sautéing, browning and setting things aside. But we discovered you can whack everything but the liquid into a baking dish, browning it all in one go. Pour the wine and stock in on top and pop it back into the oven. A much less involved dish to cook, but no less fancy to serve.

Use your largest ceramic baking dish for this.

Heat the oven to 200°C/400°F/gas mark 6. Place all the prepared vegetables in the baking dish along with the oil and some salt and pepper. Toss. Season the chicken legs all over, then place them on top of the vegetables. Scatter the bacon pieces on top of the vegetables, around the chicken.

Place in the preheated oven and roast everything together for 40 minutes, giving the vegetables a shuffle around once, halfway through.

Remove from the oven and add the wine, crushed garlic, thyme and bay leaf. Whisk a couple of tablespoons of the hot stock with the flour to form a smooth paste, then mix into the rest of the stock and pour into the dish too. Turn the chicken legs skin side down – they should be almost submerged – and place in the oven for 20 minutes. Remove from the oven again and skim off any fat that has risen to the surface. Turn the chicken back so that the skin is facing up and return to the oven for another 30–40 minutes, until the skin has crisped and the sauce has reduced.

(You shouldn't need to do this, but if the sauce is still very thin at the end of cooking, remove the chicken from the dish and set aside somewhere warm. Whisk another tablespoon of flour into a tablespoon of the hot sauce, until smooth, then stir into the liquid in the dish and cook for a further 10 minutes, without the meat. However, keep in mind that this sauce shouldn't be at all thick and gloopy, but rich and glossy.)

Serve with the fresh parsley scattered over the top and with crusty bread to mop up the sauce.

\\\\ TIP ////

Because this contains so much wine – nearly two thirds of a bottle – it pays to use something decent. Avoid anything which calls itself cooking or table wine. You don't need to spend a lot, but too cheap and it will taste it.

CRAY-CRAY

SERVES 4–6 (pictured overleaf)
PREP TIME: 30 MINS, plus 2 hours chilling · COOK TIME: 20 MINS
(WF · GF if served without bread, but check the sausage ingredients)

. . . .

We love New England-style clambakes and Louisiana-style crawfish boils, and this is our homage to them both. Often cooked outside, or on the beach, this is a scaled-down, stovetop version, but feel free to scale it up or cook it al fresco.

Place the crayfish in the freezer for 2 hours before cooking, to stun them. If cooking live crayfish is too much for you, you can use frozen crayfish or raw prawns, or increase the amount of shellfish, including different types of clams or some mussels.

. . . .

150g **sea lettuce** or other **edible seaweed** (optional)

125ml **white wine**

1 **onion**, cut into 6 wedges

1 bulb of **garlic**, halved across the middle

1 teaspoon **flaky sea salt**
(omit if using seaweed)

700g **red-skinned potatoes**,
cut into chunks

4 ears of **sweetcorn**, halved

50g **smoked sausage** or **cooking chorizo**,
chopped into 1cm pieces

3 2kg **live crayfish**

1kg **live clams**, cleaned

3 tablespoons **finely chopped fresh parsley**

2 tablespoons **finely chopped fresh tarragon**

lemon wedges, for squeezing over

TO SERVE:

crusty bread

150g **salted butter**, melted

SPICE MIX:

1 teaspoon **mild chilli flakes**

1 teaspoon **sweet paprika**

½ teaspoon **mustard powder**

¼ teaspoon **freshly ground black pepper**

¼ teaspoon **ground allspice**

a pinch of **ground ginger**

a pinch of **ground cinnamon**

a pinch of **cayenne**

a pinch of **grated nutmeg**

½ teaspoon **celery salt**
(alternatively you can use a couple of sticks of fresh celery in the broth, or a pinch of dill seed or caraway)

If using sea lettuce, rinse it well to remove any excess salt, then tie it up in a piece of muslin, otherwise it will fall apart and get all over the other ingredients.

In a truly massive pan (ours is 38cm wide and 18cm deep) with a tight-fitting lid, put the wine, onion, garlic, sea lettuce (or flaky sea salt) and potatoes, with 2 litres freshly boiled water plus a tablespoon of the spice mix. Bring back to the boil and simmer for 12 minutes.

Next, tuck the sweetcorn and sausage pieces into the broth. Then, working quickly, use tongs to place the stunned crayfish on top of the bubbling broth and cover with the lid. Turn the heat up and cook for 5 minutes. When you lift the lid the crayfish should all be bright red.

Add the clams to the pan and put the lid back on. Cook for 2 minutes, or until all the shells have opened. (Discard any that haven't opened before serving.)

Check the potatoes are tender. Then, to serve, use tongs and a slotted spoon to remove the seafood, corn, potatoes, sausage and muslin bag of seaweed, leaving the garlic and onion in the broth.

We like to serve this on newspaper, which is how such feasts are often served in the US: cover a large tray with sheets of newspaper and tip everything except the broth on to it. Scatter with the chopped herbs and squeeze the lemon juice over. Serve with crusty bread and the melted butter in a bowl, for dipping. Use a ladle to strain cupfuls of the broth out for everyone to have on the side.

TIP

We like to add seaweed because it adds a little of the flavour found in New England beach-side clambakes, where the food is cooked with layers of sea-foraged greenery. But it can be hard to find if you don't have a friendly fishmonger, so it's not essential.

CRAY-CRAY

RISOTTO 4 WAYS

COURGETTE, LEMON & PARMESAN RISOTTO

SERVES 4
PREP TIME: 15 MINS • COOK TIME: 35 MINS
WF · GF · V (if vegetarian Parmesan and vegetable stock used)

. . . .

3 tablespoons **butter**

1 **courgette**, finely diced

1 **onion**, finely diced

1 stick of **celery**, very finely diced

1 clove of **garlic**, crushed

300g **risotto rice**

125ml **white wine**

1 litre hot **chicken** or **vegetable stock**

zest of ½ **unwaxed lemon**

2 teaspoons **lemon juice**

1 tablespoon **finely chopped fresh parsley**

4 tablespoons **freshly grated Parmesan**, plus more to serve

salt and **freshly ground black pepper**

Many lemon risottos call for an egg yolk and a dollop of double cream – scrumptious but rich. We reckon creamy, mellow courgette does the trick instead. (Although if you fancy a treat, whisk a yolk and 3 tablespoons of cream together, and stir through the cooked risotto, off the heat…)

. . . .

Set a wide, deep, heavy-based pan over a medium heat. Add 1 tablespoon of the butter and, when melted, add the courgette. Sauté gently until just golden brown and beginning to soften, then lift out of the pan and set aside. Add another spoonful of butter, the onion and the celery. Sauté again, stirring often, until soft, but not browned, about 10 minutes, then add the garlic and cook for 1 minute.

Add the risotto rice to the pan and stir well, coating the rice in the butter. Cook for a couple of minutes, then add the wine. Continue to stir until all the wine has been absorbed by the rice. Slowly begin to add the hot stock, a ladleful or so at a time, waiting until all the liquid has been absorbed before adding more. You may not need all the stock; risotto should be thick and creamy, not wet and sloppy. After about 20 minutes, taste the risotto. The rice should be nicely al dente – don't cook it so long that it becomes mushy.

Remove from the heat and return the sautéed courgette to the pan to warm it through. Stir in the last spoonful of butter, the lemon zest, lemon juice, a little salt and lots of pepper, the parsley and the Parmesan. Taste, and add more seasoning, lemon juice or cheese, if needed.

Serve in wide shallow bowls, with the block of Parmesan and a grater to hand.

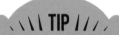

\\\ TIP ///

Risotto is an obvious home for leftover roast chicken, but we also love it with smoked fish (let about 200–250g cook in the rice) and maybe even a poached egg; broccoli and blue cheese; prawns, chorizo and smoked paprika; cooked sausage; peas and pancetta…

RISOTTO
4 WAYS

TOMATO & BASIL RISOTTO

SERVES 4
PREP TIME: 15 MINS
COOK TIME: 30 MINS
**WF · GF · V (if vegetarian Parmesan
and vegetable stock used)**

· ·

2 tablespoons **butter**

1 **onion**, finely diced

1 clove of **garlic**, crushed

2 teaspoons **tomato purée**

2 **tomatoes**, seeded and
    very finely diced

3 tablespoons **passata**

300g **risotto rice**

125ml **white wine**

1 litre hot **chicken** or **vegetable stock**

fresh basil leaves from 2 bushy sprigs,
    torn into small pieces

2 tablespoons **freshly grated Parmesan**,
    plus more to serve

salt and **freshly ground black pepper**

Set a wide, deep, heavy-based pan over a medium heat. Add 1 tablespoon of the butter and, when melted, add the onion and garlic. Sauté gently until just golden brown and beginning to soften. Add the tomato purée and cook, stirring, for 2 minutes. Add 1 of the chopped tomatoes and the passata, and cook for another 2 minutes. Add the rice and stir well, coating it in the buttery onion and tomato mixture. Cook for a couple of minutes, then add the wine. Continue to stir until all the wine has been absorbed by the rice.

Slowly begin to add the hot stock, a ladleful or so at a time, waiting until all the liquid has been absorbed before adding more. You may not need all the stock; risotto should be thick and creamy, not wet and sloppy. After about 20 minutes, taste the risotto. The rice should be nicely al dente – don't cook it so long that it becomes mushy.

When creamy, remove from the heat. Add some salt and pepper, the basil, Parmesan and the remaining butter and fresh tomato. Stir well and serve with more Parmesan shaved over the top.

RISOTTO PRIMAVERA WITH GOATS' CHEESE

SERVES 4
PREP TIME: 15 MINS
COOK TIME: 30 MINS
WF · GF · V (if vegetarian Parmesan and vegetable stock used)

. . . .

2 tablespoons **butter** or **olive oil**

1 **onion**, finely diced

1 clove of **garlic**, crushed

300g **risotto rice**

125ml **white wine**

1 litre hot **chicken** or **vegetable stock**

100g **fresh** or **frozen peas**

100g **fresh** or **frozen broad beans**, podded

100g **asparagus**, sliced into 3cm pieces

2 **spring onions**, finely diced

50g **watercress**, stems removed and discarded, leaves finely chopped (optional)

1 tablespoon **finely chopped fresh parsley**

150g **mild and creamy goats' cheese**, at room temperature, crumbled

salt and **freshly ground black pepper**

Set a wide, deep, heavy-based pan over a medium heat. Add 1 tablespoon of the butter or oil and, when melted, add the onion and garlic. Sauté gently until just golden brown and beginning to soften. Add the rice and stir well, coating it in the butter. Cook for a couple of minutes, then add the wine. Continue to stir until all the wine has been absorbed by the rice.

Slowly begin to add the hot stock, a ladleful or so at a time, waiting until all the liquid has been absorbed before adding more. You may not need all the stock; risotto should be thick and creamy, not wet and sloppy. After about 15 minutes, add the peas, broad beans, asparagus and spring onions. Continue to cook for a further 5 minutes, stirring, until the vegetables are just tender, and the risotto is creamy.

When ready, remove from the heat. Add the remaining butter or oil with the watercress, if using, parsley and some salt and pepper. Stir, taste, and add more seasoning if necessary. To serve, arrange each portion in a shallow bowl, and top with the crumbled goats' cheese and some more black pepper.

PEARL BARLEY & LEEK RISOTTO

SERVES 4
PREP TIME: 15 MINS • COOK TIME: 1 HOUR
V (if vegetarian Parmesan and vegetable stock used) • (DF • Ve if butter and Parmesan omitted)

2 tablespoons **butter** or **olive oil**

1 **onion**, finely diced

1 **leek**, finely sliced

1 clove of **garlic**, crushed

175g **pearl barley**, washed and drained

60ml **dry white wine**

450–500ml **chicken** or **vegetable stock**, made up so it's weak (and not too salty)

a handful of **fresh parsley**, finely chopped

salt

freshly grated Parmesan, to serve (optional)

Pearl barley makes a gorgeous risotto, with a firmer texture and nuttier flavour than rice (it also contains more fibre).

Put a large saucepan over a medium heat and add the butter or oil. When melted, add the onion, leek and a pinch of salt. Soften them but don't brown, stirring often, for 8 minutes, then add the garlic and cook for 1 minute longer. Add the pearl barley to the pan and cook for a couple of minutes, stirring to coat the grains in the fat, just like normal risotto. Next add the wine and let it bubble for 3 or 4 minutes.

Add 450ml of the stock a quarter at a time, waiting about 5 minutes after each addition before adding more. The last quarter should be added after roughly 20 minutes cooking time. You will need to cook the barley and stock for about another 25 minutes (45 minutes in total) in order for the barley to be tender, but not mushy. Cover with a lid and simmer very gently, stirring every now and then so it doesn't stick. Add the remaining stock if it seems dry.

When the risotto is creamy and the barley is tender, remove from the heat. Taste and correct the seasoning if necessary. Serve with the parsley stirred through and a little Parmesan grated on top, if using.

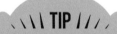

TIP

Robust barley stands up well to cured meat – sauté hunks of herby sausage or chorizo in the pan before cooking the risotto, then return it to the pot to warm through at the end. Alternatively, add 200g of cooked borlotti or cannellini beans and some thyme leaves about 5 minutes before you're ready to serve.

ROAST POUSSINS WITH BOULANGÈRE POTATOES

SERVES 4

PREP TIME: 15 MINS • COOK TIME: 1½ HOURS, plus 10 mins resting

WF · GF

3 tablespoons **olive oil**

2 **onions**, very thinly sliced

2 cloves of **garlic**, crushed

+ 2 cloves of **garlic**, peeled and whole

750g **Maris Piper potatoes**, peeled and very finely sliced

1 **bay leaf**

1 sprig of **fresh rosemary**, broken into pieces

550ml hot **chicken stock**

2 or 3 **oven-ready poussins**

a large knob of **butter**

4–6 bushy sprigs of **fresh thyme**, leaves only

4 **ripe purple figs**, quartered

salt and **freshly ground black pepper**

Boulangère means roasting layers of thinly sliced potatoes in stock, much like dauphinoise, but without the cream. Traditionally, it is either made as a side dish, or with lamb roasted on top, but we love it with poultry.

If the poussins seem small, or if you're very hungry, you should up the quantity to 4 birds, but 2 plump poussins should be enough for 4 people.

Heat the oven to 180°C/350°F/gas mark 4. Put 1 tablespoon of the oil in a large, wide ovenproof pan over a low heat. Add the onions and a pinch of salt and soften the onions for about 5 minutes; don't allow them to brown. Add the crushed garlic and cook for 1 minute. Remove the onion mixture from the pan, set aside and turn off the heat.

Add the remaining oil to the pan, swirling to coat the base and sides (to prevent the potatoes sticking). Starting with a layer of sliced raw potatoes, arrange the potatoes and cooked onions in alternate layers, seasoning with salt and pepper between the layers, and tucking in the bay leaf and rosemary along the way. Finish with a layer of potatoes, carefully covering all the onion. Pour over the hot stock – it should just cover the top layer of potatoes (add a little water if it doesn't), then slide the pan into the preheated oven and cook for 30 minutes.

Meanwhile, rub the birds all over with the butter, then season generously with salt and pepper. Tuck a whole clove of garlic and a quarter of the thyme into each of the cavities, scattering over the rest of the thyme leaves. Perch the birds on top of the potatoes and turn the oven up to 200°C/400°F/gas mark 6. Roast for 40 minutes. Finally, add the quartered figs for a final 10 minutes of cooking – they should be soft, but not collapsing.

Before serving, rest the whole dish for 10 minutes, loosely covered with foil. Turn the birds upside down as they rest to redistribute the juices and turn back to serve. Serve the poussins with the boulangère potatoes and the squidgy figs on the side.

TIP

Use ripe, fat, sweet figs for this dish (if you can't get good figs, just leave them out).

CHANTAL'S SAFFRON CHICKEN QUINOA PILAF

SERVES 4

PREP TIME: 20 MINS · COOK TIME: 25 MINS, plus 15 mins steaming

WF · GF · DF

175g **uncooked quinoa**

1 tablespoon **olive oil**

1 large **onion**, diced

6 boneless **chicken thighs**, each sliced into 3 or 4 chunks

a generous pinch of **saffron threads**

1 **cinnamon stick**

1 tablespoon **coriander seeds**

1 teaspoon **ground cumin**

6 cloves of **garlic**, crushed

1 teaspoon **grated fresh ginger**

1 **head of fennel**, finely diced

1 **carrot**, sliced into thin half-moons

375ml hot **chicken** or **vegetable stock**

100g **green beans**

100g **tenderstem** or **other long-stemmed broccoli**

100g **broad beans**

TO SERVE:

1 tablespoon **toasted hazelnuts**, roughly chopped

1 tablespoon **toasted flaked almonds**

a big handful of **fresh coriander**, roughly chopped

lemon juice

John's friend and colleague Chantal Symons invented this clever way with quinoa. This pilaf is zesty from the lemon and saffron, with crisp, just-cooked vegetables.

Rinse the quinoa under running water, then drain and set aside.

Place a large pan with a lid over a high heat. Add the oil and when hot add the onion and fry for 5 minutes. Next, add the chicken pieces, spices, garlic, ginger, fennel and carrot. Fry for another 5 minutes, stirring all the time. Add a tablespoon of water if the spices start to stick.

Add the quinoa and stir to coat, then add the hot stock. Stir again, then layer the remaining vegetables on top of the quinoa. Cover with a lid, turn the heat to high, bring to the boil, then turn the heat down and leave to simmer for 10 minutes. Then turn off the heat and leave for 15 minutes with the lid on, to steam.

Remove the cinnamon stick. To serve, top with the toasted nuts, fresh coriander and a good squeeze of lemon.

\\\ TIP ///
Rinsing quinoa before cooking ensures that any bitterness is removed.

GHORMEH SABZI

SERVES 4

PREP TIME: 25 MINS • COOK TIME: 3¼ HOURS

(WF • GF if served with rice) • DF

2 tablespoons **flavourless oil**

900g **lamb shoulder**, cut into cubes, fat and gristle trimmed

2 large **onions**, finely diced

4 cloves of **garlic**, crushed

2 teaspoons **ground turmeric**

150g **fresh** or **frozen fenugreek leaves** (not dried), finely chopped

3 large handfuls **fresh parsley**, finely chopped

3 large handfuls **fresh coriander**, finely chopped

1 large **leek**, trimmed, halved lengthwise and finely sliced

300g **fresh spinach**, finely chopped

1 × 400g can of **kidney beans**, drained and rinsed

1 large **preserved lemon**, pierced 3 or 4 times with the tip of a sharp knife

1 tablespoon **lemon juice**

salt

microwave rice or **flatbreads**, to serve

This glorious stew is one of Iran's national dishes, traditionally served with rice. The herbs and greens wilt down to create an extraordinary sauce – don't skip slow-cooking them until dark green, as it's where the wonderful distinctive flavour comes from.

If you can't find fresh fenugreek leaves, many large supermarkets and Asian food stores stock bags of frozen, chopped uncooked leaves (often called methi), which work just as well. The cooking time is long, but is mostly hands off, while the stew slowly cooks in the oven.

Heat the oven to 160°C/325°F/gas mark 3.

Place a large, wide, deep ovenproof pan with a lid over a high heat and add half the oil. Thoroughly brown the lamb in batches so that it doesn't stew. Remove the meat and set aside. Turn the heat to low and add the onions. Cook until they are just beginning to brown, about 8 minutes, then add the garlic and turmeric. Cook for 1 minute.

Next add the chopped herbs, leek and spinach to the pan and cook over a medium heat, stirring frequently, first in order to wilt the leaves, then to allow any liquid to evaporate away – this will take 5–10 minutes, depending on your pan. Finally add the remaining oil and sauté the leaves until they turn a rich dark green (but don't allow them to burn), which will take another 5–10 minutes.

Add 1 litre boiling water with a teaspoon of salt and the browned lamb to the pan, stir, then cover and place in the preheated oven. Cook for 2 hours, or until the meat is tender and beginning to fall apart.

Add the kidney beans and preserved lemon and return the pan to the oven for another 40 minutes. When the meat is meltingly tender and the tang of preserved lemon has infused into the sauce, take the dish out of the oven, remove the preserved lemon and add the lemon juice. Taste and add a little more salt or lemon juice – the dish should be slightly tart – if necessary. Serve with rice or flatbreads.

\\\\ TIP ////

If you can find dried Persian limes,
use them in place of preserved lemon
— use three and treat them exactly
the same way as the lemon, carefully
piercing their hard skins with the
prongs of a fork or a very sharp knife.
They are tart, so you may not need
any fresh lemon juice afterwards.

BAKED TERIYAKI DUCK LEGS
WITH PAK CHOY

SERVES 4

PREP TIME: 10 MINS · COOK TIME: 45 MINS, plus 5 mins resting

WF · GF (check soy sauce ingredients) · DF

4 tablespoons **soy sauce**

4 tablespoons **mirin**

4cm piece of **fresh ginger**, peeled
and grated

4 × 200–225g **whole duck legs**

450g **pak choy**, base and outer
leaves removed, and quartered

6 large **spring onions**, trimmed and
cut lengthways

salt and **freshly ground black pepper**

This easy one-tray meal requires minimal effort to put together, but your family or friends will think it was a mission.

Heat the oven to 180°C/350°F/gas mark 4.

Whisk together the soy, mirin and ginger to make a sauce. Coat the duck legs with 4 tablespoons of the sauce (a spoonful per leg), season, then place in a large ceramic baking dish and cook in the preheated oven for 35 minutes. Set aside the rest of the sauce.

Remove the duck legs from the oven and carefully drain off the excess fat (ideally, use a fat-separating jug to retain the cooking juices but remove the fat). Tuck the pak choy and spring onions around the duck legs in the baking dish. Pour half the remaining sauce over the duck legs and drizzle the rest over the pak choy and spring onions.

Return the dish to the oven for 7–9 minutes, until the pak choy has just wilted but still retains a good amount of bite.

Remove from the oven and rest the meat for 5 minutes before serving. Lift the vegetables out of the pan and keep warm, then drain off the remaining sauce, again removing the excess fat. Pour into a jug and keep warm. Serve the duck legs with the sauce and greens.

\\\\ TIP ////

You can use this teriyaki-style sauce on all kinds of things – try marinating salmon fillets in it, then pan-frying them, or use it to add a rich flavour to firm tofu.

SMOKY POUSSINS
WITH POTATO WEDGES

SERVES 4

PREP TIME: 15 MINS • COOK TIME: 45 MINS, plus 10 mins resting

WF · GF · DF

800g **Maris Piper potatoes**,
each cut into 8–10 wedges

2 **red peppers**, seeded and cut into
large chunks

8 cloves of **garlic**, in their skins

3 tablespoons **olive oil**

1 teaspoon **sherry vinegar**

salt and **freshly ground black pepper**

POUSSINS:

2 teaspoons **smoked paprika**

2 cloves of **garlic**, crushed

½ teaspoon **ground cumin**

½ teaspoon **ground coriander**

2 tablespoons **olive oil**

juice of 1 **lemon**

2 **oven-ready poussins**

salt and **freshly ground black pepper**

Instead of ordinary potatoes, you could use sweet potato. If you really want to save time, use red pepper sauce from a jar instead of making the relish yourself.

Heat the oven to 200°C/400°F/gas mark 6.

Toss the potato wedges, pepper chunks and garlic cloves in the oil with some salt and black pepper. Mix the paprika, garlic, cumin, coriander, oil and lemon juice together with a pinch of salt and some black pepper, then coat the birds with it, spooning some inside the cavities as well.

Arrange everything on one large tray in groups – peppers together, potatoes together and birds together, then roast in the preheated oven for 45 minutes, turning the vegetables and basting the meat once, halfway through.

Remove from the oven and check that the poussins are done – the juices should run clear and the meat should pull easily from the bones.

Rest the birds for 10 minutes, loosely covered in foil; keep the potato wedges warm.

Meanwhile, make the pepper relish. Chop the roasted peppers into little pieces. Squeeze the soft roasted cloves of garlic from their skins and place in a bowl with the roasted pepper and the sherry vinegar. Mash roughly, using a fork. Taste and add a little more salt, if necessary.

Serve the relish warm, alongside the poussins and the potato wedges.

\\\\ TIP ////
If you can't find poussins,
this works with bone-in chicken
joints as well.

PAELLA

SERVES 4

PREP TIME: 15 MINS · COOK TIME: 35 MINS, plus 10 mins resting

WF · GF · DF

. . . .

5 tablespoons **olive oil**

1 **onion**, finely diced

½ **red pepper**, diced

4 cloves of **garlic**, crushed

100ml **white wine**

200g **chopped tomatoes** (half a can)

a generous pinch of **saffron strands**

1 teaspoon **sweet paprika**

1 teaspoon **sweet smoked paprika**

500ml **fresh shellfish stock**

200g **paella rice**

250g **raw king prawns**,
    a mixture of shell on and off

1 medium **raw squid** (about 150g),
    cleaned and body sliced into rings

300g **uncooked clams** or a mixture
    of **clams** and **mussels**

good-quality **extra virgin olive oil**

a little **fresh lemon juice**

fresh parsley, chopped

salt and **freshly ground black pepper**

lemon wedges, to serve

Paella is perhaps the ultimate one-pot dish. Although it looks spectacular, it is pretty straightforward to make at home.

. . . .

Use a paella pan or a large, wide frying pan with a thin base and a lid.

Place the pan on the widest ring on your hob, set at a medium heat, and when hot, add the olive oil, onion and a pinch of salt. Cook, stirring, until soft and beginning to brown. Add the red pepper and, a minute later, the garlic. Cook for a further minute, then add the white wine and cook for 2 more minutes. After the wine has bubbled down a bit, add the chopped tomatoes, saffron, both kinds of paprika and a good dose of black pepper. Once bubbling, add the stock and heat until boiling.

Finally, add the rice and a further pinch of salt. Stir once, then turn the heat to medium–low and cook for 12 minutes, without stirring at all. The rice will cook in the stock. (If the rice seems to be very dry well before the cooking time has elapsed, add 50–100ml of hot water. However, bear in mind that this isn't a soupy rice dish.)

Next, again without stirring or moving the rice, add the prawns, squid and clams, carefully prodding them into the rice so that they are partially covered by the paella mixture. Cover with a lid for 3½ minutes, to help the clams cook; discard any that fail to open at the very end of the cooking process.

Remove from the heat and half cover the pan with the lid, letting the paella rest. Leave to stand for 10 minutes.

When ready to serve, taste to check the seasoning, adding more salt or pepper as necessary. Drizzle with generous amounts of extra virgin olive oil and a little fresh lemon juice, then sprinkle with parsley, and serve each portion with lemon wedges for squeezing over.

\\\\ TIP ////

You can add firm white fish,
chicken, rabbit or even chorizo
(although not true to the original)
to this paella. Sauté any fish briefly
when cooking the onions, then
remove it and return it to the pan
with the shellfish. Brown any meat
and return to the pan with the rice;
ensure that it is cooked through
before serving.

BAKED MEATBALL PASTA

SERVES 4

PREP TIME: 20 MINS • COOK TIME: 1 HOUR, plus 5 mins resting

MEATBALLS:

1 slice of **slightly stale bread**,
   torn into pieces with crusts removed

milk, for soaking

1 tablespoon **olive oil**

1 **onion**, finely chopped

500g **minced beef** (not low-fat)

¼ teaspoon **dried oregano**

2 teaspoons **fennel seeds**

3 tablespoons **freshly grated Parmesan**

2 cloves of **garlic**, minced

4 tablespoons **finely chopped**
   fresh parsley

salt and **freshly ground black pepper**

SAUCE:

20 **cherry tomatoes**, halved

3 tablespoons **olive oil**, plus more to finish

1 **aubergine**, chopped into 2cm chunks

2 tablespoons **tomato purée**

2 cloves of **garlic**, crushed

600ml **passata**

½ teaspoon **dried oregano**

4 sprigs of **fresh basil leaves**,
   roughly torn

325g **medium-sized pasta**,
   such as **rigatoni**

1 ball of **mozzarella**

3 tablespoons **freshly grated Parmesan**

salt and **freshly ground black pepper**

This is a family favourite in Rebecca's house. Kids can get involved in the cooking – enlist them to help shape the meatballs. The pasta cooks in the sauce, so there's no need to parboil it.

Put the bread into a shallow bowl, pour over a little milk to soften it and set aside. Pour the oil into a large, wide ovenproof pan with a lid. Set over a medium heat and add the onion and a pinch of salt. Cook, stirring, for about 5 minutes, until the onion begins to soften. Remove it from the pan and place half in a bowl with the remaining meatball ingredients. Mix together using your hands, but stop once it's just combined, as over-working will make the meatballs tough.

Return the pan to the heat and fry a little nugget to check the seasoning. When happy, shape into 16 equally sized meatballs. Brown the meatballs all over (add a little extra oil if the pan seems dry), turning them two or three times. Remove from the pan and set aside. Meanwhile, heat the oven to 200°C/400°F/gas mark 6.

For the sauce, return the remaining softened onion to the pan along with the cherry tomatoes. Cook until the tomatoes are collapsing, about 8–10 minutes, then add the rest of the oil and the aubergine. After 3 or 4 minutes, add the tomato purée and crushed garlic and cook, stirring all the time, for a couple of minutes. Next, add the passata, oregano and half the basil. Season, then stir and bring up to a simmer. Taste and add more seasoning if necessary.

Add the dried pasta and 500ml boiling water – it should be enough to almost cover the pasta, add more if not. Return to a simmer, then cover the pan and place in the oven. Cook for 15 minutes, then remove from the oven, stir once and half submerge the meatballs in the sauce. Cover and return to the oven for a further 10 minutes.

Remove from the oven and check that the meatballs are cooked through. Tear the mozzarella into strips and arrange on top of the pasta and meatballs, then sprinkle over the Parmesan. Return to the oven for about 10 minutes, or until the cheese has melted and is beginning to brown. Let stand for 5 minutes before serving. Serve with the remaining basil leaves scattered over the dish.

FREEKEH MUJADARA

SERVES 2

PREP TIME: 15 MINS • COOK TIME: 35 MINS

V • (DF • Ve if served with non-dairy yoghurt)

. . . .

1 tablespoon **olive oil**

2 **onions**, finely sliced

2 cloves of **garlic**, crushed

½ teaspoon **ground cumin**

½ teaspoon **ground coriander**

a pinch of **ground allspice**

250g **ready-cooked green lentils**

150g **ready-cooked freekeh**

salt and **freshly ground black pepper**

TO SERVE:

4 heaped tablespoons **thick Greek-style
   yoghurt** or **non-dairy yoghurt**

chopped fresh parsley or **coriander**,
   or both

*Mujadara is a mixed rice and lentil dish topped with crispy onions
– versions of it exist in Greece and across the Middle East. We enjoy
making it with ready-cooked freekeh instead of rice. Freekeh is a toasted
green wheat with a nutty, slightly smoky flavour, which you can buy in
vacuum packs in large supermarkets.*

. . . .

Set a wide frying pan over a low heat and add the oil. When hot, add the sliced
onions and cook slowly, stirring often, for about 25 minutes, or until caramelized,
deep brown and beginning to crisp up. Remove half the onions and set aside. Add
1 garlic clove and cook for 1 minute, then add the cumin, coriander and allspice, stir
and cook for a minute longer.

Now add the lentils, freekeh, some salt and pepper, and 200ml hot water and
simmer briefly, just for 3 or 4 minutes, to let the flavours come together and heat
everything through.

Meanwhile stir the remaining clove of garlic into the yoghurt along with a pinch
of salt.

Serve the mujadara topped with the garlic yoghurt, the remaining crispy onions and
the fresh herbs.

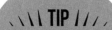

\\\ TIP ///

Most ready-cooked freekeh comes
in 250g packets – use the leftover
grains in a salad, with cucumber,
tomatoes, parsley and mint.

HERBY CHEESY SWEET POTATOES

SERVES 2
PREP TIME: 10 MINS • COOK TIME: 45 MINS
WF · GF · V

4 medium **sweet potatoes**

olive oil

2 heaped tablespoons **very finely chopped fresh chives**

2 heaped tablespoons **very finely chopped fresh parsley**

200g **feta**, at room temperature

salt and **freshly ground black pepper**

In the depths of winter, a vivid orange sweet potato acts like a dose of sunshine. (It also contains buckets of vitamin A, among all sorts of other nutritional goodies.) A spud-you'll-love.

Heat the oven to 200°C/400°F/gas mark 6.

Rub each potato with olive oil and season all over with salt and pepper. Prick the skin once or twice with a fork. Arrange on a baking sheet or tray.

Slide the tray into the preheated oven and cook for 45 minutes, or until the potatoes offer no resistance to the point of a sharp knife.

While the potatoes are cooking, mash the herbs into the cheese along with some more black pepper.

Remove the potatoes from the oven and cut a cross into each one. Open slightly and stuff each potato with a quarter of the herbed cheese mixture. (If you want the cheese to warm a little, return to the oven for 3 or 4 minutes.) Drizzle with a little extra olive oil and eat while hot.

TIP

Instead of feta, try rindless goats' cheese, or use full-fat cream cheese and add some dill. If you love chilli, add some finely chopped fresh or crumbled dried red chilli to the cheese as well. If you happen to have some toasted seeds or nuts to hand, they would add a lovely bit of crunch.

BAKED CHICKEN CURRY

SERVES 4

PREP TIME: 20 MINS • COOK TIME: 1 HOUR

• •

3 tablespoons **flavourless oil**

4–8 skin-on, bone-in **chicken thighs**, depending on your hunger

200g **cauliflower**, broken into florets

200g **cherry tomatoes**, halved

1 large **onion**, finely sliced

1 × 4cm piece of **fresh ginger**, peeled and grated

1 teaspoon **mustard seeds**

½ teaspoon **ground turmeric**

½ teaspoon **ground coriander**

½ teaspoon **cumin seeds**

6 **cardamom pods**

2 cloves of **garlic**, crushed

8 **curry leaves**

2 tablespoons seeded and finely chopped **green chilli**

¼ teaspoon **cayenne**

3 tablespoons **full-fat Greek-style yoghurt**

a handful of **fresh coriander leaves**

salt and **freshly ground black pepper**

TO SERVE:

warm **Indian flatbreads**

Indian pickles

Throw it all into a tray and chuck it into the oven – resulting in a beautifully spiced chicken curry.

• •

Heat the oven to 200°C/400°F/gas mark 6.

Use a large, deep metal baking tray. In it, place the oil, chicken, cauliflower, tomatoes, onion, ginger, mustard seeds, turmeric, ground coriander, cumin seeds and cardamom pods, plus ½ teaspoon of salt and some freshly ground black pepper. Toss well to coat everything in the oil and spices.

Slide the tray into the preheated oven and cook for 25 minutes, turning everything once halfway through.

Take the dish out of the oven, remove the cauliflower and set aside. Add the garlic, curry leaves, chilli and cayenne to the pan along with 200ml boiling water and return it to the oven for 30 minutes. Check the chicken is cooked through – the meat should pull easily from the bones and the juices should run clear. Return the cauliflower to the pan, stir, then put back into the oven for 5 minutes. Stir the yoghurt and coriander leaves through just before serving.

Eat with warm flatbreads and Indian pickles.

HERBY SAUSAGES WITH LENTILS & CABBAGE

SERVES 2

PREP TIME: 5 MINS · COOK TIME: 22 MINS

WF · GF (check sausage ingredients) · DF

- a splash of **olive oil**
- 4–6 **herby sausages**, depending on their size and your hunger
- 1 **leek**, finely sliced
- 150ml hot **vegetable stock**
- 250g **ready-cooked green lentils**
- 1 sprig of **fresh rosemary**
- 1 clove of **garlic**, whole, bruised with the flat of a knife
- 150g **green cabbage** (**hispi**, **sweetheart**, **kale** or **spring greens**), shredded

Rebecca's neighbour Tracy – a brilliant cook – swears by adding a handful of cherry tomatoes to this, once the sausages are browned.

Set a large frying pan with a lid over a medium heat. When hot, pour in a splash of oil and add the sausages and leek. Gently brown the sausages all over (keeping the heat low or the skins may split) while the leek softens in the pan. Next, add the hot vegetable stock and the cooked lentils, along with the rosemary and garlic. Bring to a simmer and cook for 10 minutes, or until the stock has reduced a little and the sausages are done. Finally, add the shredded cabbage, stir, and cook for another 2 minutes – the cabbage should still have plenty of bite. Remove the garlic and rosemary before serving.

Serve in shallow bowls to contain the pan juices.

\\\\ TIP ////

We love herby sausages with earthy lentils, but you could use any kind of sausage in this dish.

CHORIZO & CHICKPEA STEW

SERVES 4 (generously)
PREP TIME: 15 MINS • COOK TIME: 40 MINS
WF • GF (check chorizo ingredients) • DF

a splash of **vegetable oil**

400g **cooking chorizo**, sliced into
   1cm chunks

2 **onions**, finely diced

1 **long red pepper**, seeded and chopped
   into small chunks

1 clove of **garlic**, crushed

2 teaspoons **sweet** or **hot**
   smoked paprika

2 × 400g cans of **chopped tomatoes**
   (or use **passata** if you prefer
   a smoother sauce)

2 × 400g cans of **chickpeas**, drained
   and rinsed

salt and **freshly ground black pepper**

TO SERVE:

a handful of **roughly chopped**
   fresh coriander

crusty bread or **toast** (optional)

This will be appearing on the LEON menu soon.

Place a large, wide, high-sided pan with a lid over a medium heat and add a tiny splash of cooking oil – the sausage will release plenty of fat, so you barely need any. Add the chorizo and brown thoroughly all over, until really well caramelized. (Work in batches if necessary, to avoid crowding the pan and stewing the meat.) Remove and set aside, leaving the red fat behind in the pan.

Add the onions and red pepper, and sauté until soft, about 10 minutes. Next add the garlic and paprika and cook, stirring, for a minute or two. Add the tomatoes and enough hot water to loosen the stew so that it doesn't dry out during cooking. Bring to a simmer, cover partially with a lid, then turn the heat down and let it bubble for 15 minutes.

Add the chickpeas to the pan along with the cooked chorizo, stir and heat through.

Serve topped with the coriander, and with a hunk of crusty bread or toast for mopping up the sauce.

\\\ TIP ///

Switch the chickpeas for cannellini beans and, for an even heartier meal, drop a couple of eggs into the finished stew and allow them to poach in the simmering sauce. Vegetarians and vegans can skip the chorizo but add extra smoked paprika.

BAKED CHICKEN PILAF WITH POMEGRANATE

SERVES 4

PREP TIME: 15 MINS • COOK TIME: 30 MINS, plus 5 mins resting

WF • GF

400g **long-grain rice**

8 skin-on, bone-in **chicken thighs**

a splash of **vegetable oil**

3 **onions**, chopped into thin wedges

6 cloves of **garlic**, peeled and bruised

10 **cardamom pods**

3 tablespoons **flaked almonds**

3 tablespoons **pine nuts**

a knob of **butter**

1 litre **chicken stock**

a generous pinch of **saffron threads**

salt and **freshly ground black pepper**

TO SERVE:

5 tablespoons **pomegranate seeds**

fresh coriander leaves

Greek-style yoghurt

On the plate, this pilaf looks more fancy than it really is, with pretty pomegranate seeds scattered over. The rice cooks in the juices from the chicken, as well as fragrant saffron and cardamom.

Washing and soaking the rice can seem like a faff, but it stops the rice becoming sticky and clumping together during cooking – in a good pilaf, you can see each individual grain of rice.

Heat the oven to 180°C/350°F/gas mark 4.

Wash the rice in three changes of water, then leave to soak in a bowl of cold water.

Season the chicken all over with salt and pepper. Set a wide, large ovenproof casserole dish with a lid over a high heat. Add a splash of oil and brown the chicken all over. Lift the meat out, set aside, and add the onions and garlic to the pan. Brown them until they just begin to char, but don't let them scorch. Add the cardamom pods, almonds, pine nuts and butter, toast the nuts for a couple of minutes, then drain the rice and add it to the pan. Add the stock and saffron threads. Stir well, then return the chicken to the pan, resting it on top of the rice and onion mixture.

Cover with the lid and place in the preheated oven. Cook for 20 minutes, by which time the chicken will have cooked through and the rice will have absorbed all the liquid. Remove from the oven and leave to rest for 5 minutes, with the lid partly on.

Serve each portion topped with the pomegranate seeds and coriander, with a dollop of yoghurt on the side.

\\\\ TIP ////

This pilaf is just as good without
the meat – try serving it with grilled
fish or roasted vegetables.

ONE-TRAY SAUSAGE & MASH

SERVES 4

PREP TIME: 15 MINS • COOK TIME: 1¾ HOURS

- 1kg large **white baking potatoes**
- 8–12 **pork sausages**, depending on their size and your hunger
- 3 tablespoons **olive oil**
- 3 **onions**, very finely sliced
- a knob of **butter**
- a splash of **milk**
- 2 teaspoons **plain flour**
- 250ml **red wine**
- 1 teaspoon **smooth Dijon mustard**
- 3 dashes of **Worcestershire sauce**
- 1 teaspoon **soy sauce**
- 400–600ml good-quality **beef or chicken stock**
- **salt** and **freshly ground black pepper**

A fuss-free way to make sausages, mash and gravy in one tray and no saucepans. Oven-baking the potatoes results in very fluffy, creamy mash.

You could speed this up by microwaving the potatoes to start their cooking process. Blast them on full power for 10 minutes, turning them once halfway through, and omit the first 50 minutes cooking time.

Heat the oven to 180°C/350°F/gas mark 4. Prick the potatoes all over with a fork. Place in the oven, directly on the oven shelf or rack, and bake for 50 minutes.

When the potatoes have been cooking for 50 minutes in the oven (or had 10 minutes in the microwave), prick the sausages once or twice with a fork. Choose a large oven tray with high sides and grease it with 1 tablespoon of oil. Add the onions and then the sausages, then pour the remaining oil over, plus some salt and pepper. Toss, then spread the onions out in a thin layer with the sausages on top. Bake for 40 minutes, turning the onions and sausages twice. (Check the onions at the edge aren't burning.)

After the 40 minutes (so the potatoes have had 90 minutes in the oven), remove the potatoes and check for done-ness by inserting a sharp knife – it should meet no resistance. (If they need longer, return them to the oven for 10–15 minutes.) When cooked, halve the potatoes, scrape out the insides and mash with the butter, milk and salt and pepper, to taste. Keep warm until ready to serve.

The sausages and potatoes should be ready at about the same time. When the sausages are brown all over and the onions are sticky, soft and brown, add the flour, wine, mustard, Worcestershire sauce and soy sauce to the pan with enough stock to make a loose sauce. Mix well, then put the pan back into the oven for 10–15 minutes to reduce the gravy and bubble off the wine. (Keep an eye on the liquid levels and top up with more stock if it reduces too fast.)

Serve the sausages resting on the warm, creamy mash, with the onion gravy poured on top.

TIP

You can save the potato skins and crisp them up in the oven with a little salt and pepper – serve them as a snack, loaded with cream cheese and chopped chives.

SAUSAGE, BRUSSELS & TAGLIATELLE

SERVES 2

PREP TIME: 15 MINS • COOK TIME: 15 MINS

. . . .

200g good-quality **Italian-style sausages** or **sausage meat**

a splash of **olive oil**

200g **Brussels sprouts**, core trimmed off, sliced

1 clove of **garlic**, bruised

150g **fresh egg tagliatelle**

3 heaped tablespoons **double cream**

2 teaspoons **Dijon mustard**

a pinch of **dried chilli flakes**

1 small bunch of **fresh basil**

salt and **freshly ground black pepper**

Cooked briefly and allowed to caramelize slightly, the unfairly maligned Brussels sprout ends up sweet and crunchy.

. . . .

Place a large, wide pan over a medium heat. If using sausages, split the skins and remove the sausage meat, then crumble the sausage meat into small pieces. Add a splash of oil to the pan and, when hot, add the meat. Cook, stirring to break up the meat still further, until beginning to brown, then add the sliced Brussels sprouts and the bruised clove of garlic and cook for 3 or 4 minutes longer, until the meat is cooked through and the sprouts are beginning to caramelize and wilt very slightly.

Add the pasta and 250ml hot water to the pan, cover and cook for 3 minutes. Next add the cream, mustard, chilli flakes, a little salt and a lot of black pepper – taste and add more seasoning or chilli, if you like. If the sauce seems too dry, add a splash of water. Just before serving, tear up the basil leaves and stir through.

CHICKEN & SPRING VEGETABLE POT PIE

SERVES 2

PREP TIME: 20 MINS • COOK TIME: 1 HOUR, plus 5 mins standing

a splash of **flavourless oil**

400g skinless, boneless **chicken thighs**, cut into bite-sized pieces

1 **large leek**, finely sliced

1 × 320g sheet of ready-rolled **all-butter puff pastry**

40g **butter**, plus more for greasing

40g **plain flour**

500ml hot **chicken** or **vegetable stock**

a dash of **Worcestershire sauce** (optional)

2 tablespoons **finely chopped fresh parsley**

2 tablespoons **roughly chopped fresh tarragon**

75g **spring greens**, shredded

1 **egg**, beaten

salt and **freshly ground black pepper**

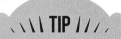

\\\\ TIP ////

Instead of greens, slice 6 asparagus spears into short lengths and add to the pie; in winter use cooked carrots and shredded kale or sliced broccoli.

A quick and easy pot pie made in a frying pan.

You can use chicken breasts if you prefer, but we think thigh meat has more flavour (plus it is usually cheaper).

Use a wide, shallow ovenproof frying pan for this – the pie cooks in the pan, so the filling should almost fill the pan when everything is added.

Set the pan over a medium heat and pour in a splash of oil. Add the chicken and brown it all over (do this in batches if necessary, so that the meat browns rather than stewing in its juices). Remove and set aside. Turn the heat to low. Add the leek to the pan with a pinch of salt and cook gently until just soft, about 5 minutes. Remove and set aside with the chicken. Meanwhile, remove the puff pastry sheet from the fridge and heat the oven to 180°C/350°F/gas mark 4.

Put the butter into the pan and, when melted, add the flour. Cook, stirring, for a couple of minutes, then slowly begin to add the hot stock, a ladleful at a time, only adding more when the flour mixture has absorbed all the liquid (don't rush this stage).

Remove from the heat. Add the Worcestershire sauce, if using, plus the parsley and tarragon. Taste and add some pepper and more salt, if necessary. Return the chicken and leeks to the pan, then add the shredded greens.

Grease the rim of the pan with a little butter. To top the pie, cut a circle out of the pastry sheet measuring roughly 4cm wider than the pan. Lay the pastry on top of the pan and brush with the beaten egg. Cut 2 small slits in the top with a sharp knife so that the steam can escape. (You could use offcuts of pastry to create a pattern on top of the pie.) Cook in the preheated oven for 40 minutes, or until the pastry lid is puffed up and golden brown.

Let stand for 5 minutes before serving.

MUSHROOM & SPINACH POT PIE

SERVES 2

PREP TIME: 20 MINS • COOK TIME: 55 MINS

V

· ·

1 × 320g sheet of ready-rolled **all-butter puff pastry**

a knob of **salted butter**, plus 2 tablespoons and more for greasing

1 **leek**, finely sliced

1 **onion**, diced

250g **mushrooms** (any kind will work here), chopped into bite-sized pieces

2 tablespoons **plain flour**

200ml hot **vegetable stock**

100g **frozen chopped spinach**

1 clove of **garlic**, crushed (optional)

1 tablespoon **chopped fresh parsley**

1 **egg**, beaten

salt and **freshly ground black pepper**

green salad, to serve (optional)

\\\\ TIP ////

It's easy to forget, but the handle of your pan will be very hot when it comes out of the oven – we speak from experience! So wrap a tea towel around it to take it out and keep it there until the pan is cool.

A veg-filled frying-pan pie.

· ·

Remove the puff pastry sheet from the fridge about 15 minutes before the pie is due to go into the oven. Heat the oven to 180°C/350°F/gas mark 4 at the same time.

Melt the knob of butter in a medium ovenproof frying pan (with a diameter of 20–25cm) over a low heat. When foaming, add the leek and onion and cook gently, without colouring, for about 6 minutes. Push the onion mixture to one side and add the mushrooms to the pan. Sauté gently until just beginning to brown. Add the rest of the butter to the pan and, when melted, add the flour. Stir to coat everything, then sauté for a couple of minutes.

Slowly add the hot stock, a few tablespoons at a time, stirring to form a sauce for the pie. When all the liquid has been added, put the frozen spinach into the pan and melt it into the sauce. Add the garlic, if using, and the parsley. Cook for 2 minutes, stirring again, then taste and add salt, if necessary, and plenty of freshly ground black pepper.

Remove the pan from the heat and grease the rim of the pan with a little butter. To top the pie, cut a circle out of the pastry sheet measuring roughly 4cm wider than the pan. Lay the pastry on top of the pan and brush with the beaten egg. Cut two small slits in the top with a sharp knife so that the steam can escape. (You could use offcuts of pastry to create a pattern on top of the pie.)

Place in the preheated oven and cook for 25–30 minutes, or until the pastry has puffed up and is a rich golden brown. Serve, if liked, with a crisp green salad.

PAN
PIZZAS
4 WAYS

There are several advantages to making pizza in a pan rather than in the oven: you don't need a pizza stone or to heat your oven to its highest temperature for an hour before cooking; they cook incredibly quickly; and the dough will spring, bubble and char just as it would in a pizza oven.

The recipe for pizza dough belongs to Rebecca's husband, Steven (also the photographer behind the pics in this book). He's been working on his pizza dough recipe for a few years now, and we think he has perfected it. He cooks his in a very hot oven on a pizza stone, but we discovered that it works for frying pan pizzas too. Alternatively, use good-quality frozen, ready-made dough, available from larger supermarkets and online. (This recipe won't work with ready-rolled bases.)

It is crucial to have all your toppings at room temperature, otherwise they won't cook quickly enough and any raw toppings will taste cold and bland when added to a hot pizza.

Because you are cooking in a pan rather than under heat coming from above, the cheese won't bubble or brown in quite the same way as a traditional pizza, so you need to pick cheeses which remain quite firm when heated (like feta) or toppings which are added raw after cooking (like buffalo mozzarella or Parma ham). If you're dying for bubbling, melted mozzarella, use grated firm mozzarella (not buffalo, which will weep water) and pop the half-cooked pizza under a very hot grill to finish.

You will need a wide frying pan, which is 25–30cm across, with a lid.

\\\\ TIP ////

Once you've mastered this easy pizza recipe, the topping possibilities are endless. The following all work, cooked under the lid: figs (add Parma ham and/ or blue cheese after cooking); boquerones (anchovies) and capers; roasted red peppers and aubergines with ricotta. Raw toppings can be added to the basic Margarita pizza: goats' curd, smoked mozzarella, or rocket and Parmesan shavings.

PIZZA DOUGH

MAKES 4 × 22cm round pizzas
PREP TIME: 20 MINS, plus 4–6 hours rising and proving
DF · V · Ve

. . . .

*If you are ever in London, come and check out
FLATPLANET®, John's little pizza place at the top of
Carnaby Street. In the meantime, try this.*

. . . .

250ml **lukewarm water**
2 teaspoons **dried yeast**
1 teaspoon **sugar**
2 tablespoons **olive oil**
475g **strong white bread flour**, plus more for dusting
1 teaspoon **fine salt**

Mix together the water, yeast and sugar. Leave to stand for
10 minutes; it will develop a frothy head. Add the olive oil,
then mix with the flour and salt. Using your hands, work the
mixture until it forms a rough dough, then continue to work it
until it becomes smooth. Flour a clean work surface, turn the
dough out on to it, and knead for 5 minutes, by which time it
should feel soft and elastic.

Oil a bowl, tip the dough ball into it, and cover with clingfilm.
Set aside for at least 4 hours to rise, ideally 6. Knock back the
dough by punching it with your knuckles, then divide it into
4 equally sized balls. Set aside to prove for 20 minutes or so,
until ready to cook.

MARINARA SAUCE

MAKES enough for 4 pizzas
PREP TIME: 5 MINS
WF · GF · DF · V · Ve

. . . .

*This sauce forms the topping for each of the following
pizzas. Any leftovers can be frozen to use on future
pizzas, or as a pasta sauce.*

. . . .

200ml **passata**
½ teaspoon **dried oregano**
1 clove of **garlic**, crushed
1 tablespoon **extra virgin olive oil**
freshly ground black pepper

Mix together all the ingredients and set aside until ready
to use.

BUFFALO MOZZARELLA & BASIL PIZZA

MAKES 2 pizzas

PREP TIME: 15 MINS, plus dough-making • COOK TIME: 11 MINS per pizza

V

2 balls proved **pizza dough** (see page 139)

2–3 tablespoons **marinara sauce**
(see page 139)

100g **firm mozzarella**, shredded
(at room temperature)

1 ball of **buffalo mozzarella**
(at room temperature), ripped into
small pieces

3 sprigs of **fresh basil**, leaves only, torn

1 tablespoon **extra virgin olive oil**

salt and **freshly ground black pepper**

Place a wide pan, ideally 30cm across, over a high heat. Leave to get really hot for about 10 minutes.

Take one ball of proved dough and use your hands to begin stretching it, in mid-air. (This technique results in a more rustic-looking pizza – if you use a rolling pin, you won't get much crust and the cooked dough will be very flat). Work around the dough, holding it lightly, using the backs of your hands to support it, and rotating it quickly over your hands, stretching each section by letting its own weight pull it downwards. Some parts will be thinner than others; don't worry. A thicker rim for the crust will naturally form as you turn the dough. If any holes appear, just pinch the dough back together.

Carefully lay the dough in the hot pan. Cook for 2–3 minutes, until bubbles begin to form on the surface of the pizza (the dough will still look uncooked). Using a large spatula and tongs, flip the pizza and cook the top for about 5 minutes, until the bubbles begin to char. Flip it back so the charred bubbles are facing upwards.

Slide the pizza on to a plate and add the toppings to the charred side: smear over a very thin layer of the marinara sauce, spreading it with the back of a spoon, then scatter over half the firm mozzarella. Slide back into the hot pan, cover with a lid, and cook for 2–3 minutes, until the cheese has melted.

Remove from the pan and top with half the buffalo mozzarella and a handful of torn basil leaves. Repeat with the second pizza.

Drizzle over a little extra virgin olive oil plus some salt and pepper, and serve each pizza straight away.

CHICORY & GOATS' CHEESE PIZZA

MAKES 2 pizzas

PREP TIME: 15 MINS, plus dough-making • COOK TIME: 11 MINS per pizza

V

1 **head of chicory**, broken into leaves, core discarded

2 teaspoons **lemon juice**

2 tablespoons **extra virgin olive oil**

2 balls proved **pizza dough** (see page 139)

2–3 tablespoons **marinara sauce** (see page 139)

200g **goats' cheese** (at room temperature)

1 heaped tablespoon **pine nuts**

salt and **freshly ground black pepper**

Place a wide pan, ideally 30cm across, over a high heat. Leave to get really hot for about 10 minutes.

Toss the chicory with the lemon juice, salt, pepper and 1 tablespoon of the oil.

Take one ball of proved dough and use your hands to begin stretching it, in mid-air. (This technique results in a more rustic-looking pizza – if you use a rolling pin, you won't get much crust and the cooked dough will be very flat). Work around the dough, holding it lightly, using the backs of your hands to support it, and rotating it quickly over your hands, stretching each section by letting its own weight pull it downwards. Some parts will be thinner than others; don't worry. A thicker rim for the crust will naturally form as you turn the dough. If any holes appear, just pinch the dough back together.

Carefully lay the dough in the hot pan. Cook for 2–3 minutes, until bubbles begin to form on the surface of the pizza (the dough will still look uncooked). Using a large spatula and tongs, flip the pizza and cook the top for about 5 minutes, until the bubbles begin to char. Flip it back so the charred bubbles are facing upwards.

Slide the pizza on to a plate and add the toppings to the charred side: smear over half the marinara sauce, spreading it thinly with the back of a spoon, then scatter over half the goats' cheese, chicory and pine nuts. Slide back into the hot pan, cover with a lid, and cook for 2–3 minutes, until the cheese has melted. Repeat with the second pizza.

Drizzle over the remaining extra virgin olive oil, and serve each pizza straight away.

ARTICHOKE & SALAMI PIZZA

MAKES 2 pizzas

PREP TIME: 15 MINS, plus dough-making • COOK TIME: 2 MINS, plus 11 MINS per pizza

8 slices of **salami**, torn into 2cm strips

2 balls proved **pizza dough** (see page 139)

2–3 tablespoons **marinara sauce**
(see page 139)

125g **firm mozzarella**, shredded
(at room temperature)

8 **artichoke hearts** from jar, quartered
(at room temperature)

1 tablespoon **extra virgin olive oil**

Place a wide pan, ideally 30cm across, over a high heat. Leave to get really hot for about 10 minutes.

When the pan for the pizzas is hot, fry the salami in it quickly, until crisp – it will only take a minute or two. Remove and set aside. (Wipe the fat from the pan – or leave it, if you prefer!)

Take one ball of proved dough and use your hands to begin stretching it, in mid-air. (This technique results in a more rustic-looking pizza – if you use a rolling pin, you won't get much crust and the cooked dough will be very flat). Work around the dough, holding it lightly, using the backs of your hands to support it, and rotating it quickly over your hands, stretching each section by letting its own weight pull it downwards. Some parts will be thinner than others; don't worry. A thicker rim for the crust will naturally form as you turn the dough. If any holes appear, just pinch the dough back together.

Carefully lay the dough in the hot pan. Cook for 2–3 minutes, until bubbles begin to form on the surface of the pizza (the dough will still look uncooked). Using a large spatula and tongs, flip the pizza and cook the top for about 5 minutes, until the bubbles begin to char. Flip it back so the charred bubbles are facing upwards.

Slide the pizza on to a plate and add the toppings to the charred side: smear half the marinara sauce thinly over the base, then scatter over half the cheese, artichoke hearts and crisp salami. Slide back into the hot pan, cover with a lid, and cook for 2–3 minutes, just until the cheese has melted. Repeat with the second pizza.

Drizzle over a little extra virgin olive oil and serve each pizza straight away.

COURGETTE, FETA & CHILLI PIZZA

MAKES 2 pizzas

PREP TIME: 15 MINS (plus dough-making) • COOK TIME: 11 MINS per pizza

V

- 2 balls proved **pizza dough** (see page 139)
- 2–3 tablespoons **marinara sauce** (see page 139)
- ½ **courgette**, shaved into ribbons, seedy middle section discarded
- 100g **feta** (at room temperature)
- 1 teaspoon **Urfa chilli flakes** (or other **mild** or **smoky chilli flakes**)
- 1 tablespoon **extra virgin olive oil**

Place a wide pan, ideally 30cm across, over a high heat. Leave to get really hot for about 10 minutes.

Take one ball of proved dough and use your hands to begin stretching it, in mid-air. (This technique results in a more rustic-looking pizza – if you use a rolling pin, you won't get much crust and the cooked dough will be very flat). Work around the dough, holding it lightly, using the backs of your hands to support it, and rotating it quickly over your hands, stretching each section by letting its own weight pull it downwards. Some parts will be thinner than others; don't worry. A thicker rim for the crust will naturally form as you turn the dough. If any holes appear, just pinch the dough back together.

Carefully lay the dough in the hot pan. Cook for 2–3 minutes, until bubbles begin to form on the surface of the pizza (the dough will still look uncooked). Using a large spatula and tongs, flip the pizza and cook the top for about 5 minutes, until the bubbles begin to char. Flip it back so the charred bubbles are facing upwards.

Slide the pizza on to a plate and add the toppings to the charred side: smear the marinara sauce thinly over the base, then scatter over half the courgette ribbons, feta and chilli flakes. Slide it back into the hot pan, cover with a lid, and cook for 2–3 minutes longer. Remove from the pan and drizzle with a little extra virgin olive oil before serving.

THREE-CHEESE STOVE-TOP MACARONI CHEESE

SERVES 4
PREP TIME: 5 MINS • COOK TIME: 35 MINS

V

- 25g **butter**
- 25g **plain flour**
- 900ml **milk**
- 300g **dried macaroni** (ideally **elbow macaroni**)
- 125g **mature Cheddar**, grated, plus more to top
- 50g **Taleggio**, crumbled into 1cm pieces
- 125g **mozzarella**, torn into small pieces
- **salt** and **freshly ground pepper**

This is a hybrid of American-style boxed mac 'n' cheese, which is made in a saucepan, and baked macaroni cheese. The pasta cooks in the béchamel sauce, then the top crisps up under the grill. The advantage is that it is quicker and uses fewer pans than old-school mac 'n' cheese, but you still get the wonderful, bubbly, browned cheese crust. (Of course, if you love boxed mac 'n' cheese, don't bother with the grilling stage.)

Always add cheese to sauces off the heat – boiling cheese will make the fat and proteins split, giving you a slightly gritty sauce.

Use a large, wide ovenproof pan with a lid. Set over a low heat. Melt the butter and, when foaming, add the flour. Mix the two together and cook, stirring, for 3 minutes. Gradually add about 200ml of the milk, a few tablespoonfuls at a time to start with, until you have a smooth, thick sauce. Add another 500ml of the milk, turn the heat to medium and bring up to a simmer, stirring. At this stage, the sauce will be very, very thin.

Add the macaroni and cook in the béchamel for 15–18 minutes, stirring every few minutes to stop the pasta sticking to itself or the sauce sticking to the bottom of the pan. The sauce will quickly thicken up.

Heat the grill.

Add the final 200ml of milk to loosen the sauce again. Remove from the heat and add the grated Cheddar. Stir until smooth, then add the other cheeses. This time, stir gently to distribute, but not too thoroughly – you want little nuggets of cheese to remain in the sauce.

Top with a final handful of grated Cheddar and place under the hot grill for 5 minutes, or until bubbling and golden brown.

\\\\ TIP ////

Pimp your mac 'n' cheese: add sliced jalapeño chilli peppers to the mix before grilling, or a dusting of smoked paprika, or a spoonful of chipotle sauce, or stir through some cooked spinach, mushrooms, sausages or bacon.

RINKU'S KHITCHURI

SERVES 4–6

PREP TIME: 20 MINS, plus 30 mins soaking • COOK TIME: 1 HOUR 10 MINS

WF · GF · V

- 175g **mixed wild** and **basmati rice** (available as a mix in most supermarkets)
- 50g **red split lentils**
- 50g **pigeon peas** (aka **gungo peas**, or use **dried green mung beans**)
- 1 tablespoon **vegetable oil**
- ½ tablespoon **ghee**
- 2 **bay leaves**
- 4 **cloves**
- 3 **cardamom pods**
- 1 **cinnamon stick**
- 1½ teaspoons **cumin seeds**
- 1 **bird's-eye chilli**, sliced lengthways (optional, remove the seeds if you prefer less heat)
- 1 medium **onion**, finely chopped
- 3 cloves of **garlic**, finely grated
- 50g **yellow split lentils**
- 2 medium **tomatoes**, seeded and chopped
- 1 teaspoon **ground turmeric**
- 2 tablespoons finely grated **fresh ginger**
- 100g **frozen petit pois**
- ½ teaspoon **sugar**
- 1 teaspoon **asafoetida**
- **fine salt**

Rinku Dutt is one of Rebecca's friends, and runs a Kolkata street food pop-up called Raastawala. Rinku says, 'Khitchuri (sometimes called khichdi, in some parts of India) is a traditional Ayurvedic dish made of rice and lentils, known for its ability to detox the body. For me, it holds vivid, fond memories of monsoons and the festive season in Kolkata. Traditionally cooked with one type of lentil, the savoury porridge-type dish has a special place in most Bengalis' hearts. I've adapted my family's recipe slightly, to use three different lentils and wild rice mixed with basmati. Khitchuri was the inspiration for the Anglo-Indian dish called kedgeree.'

Place the rice and red split lentils in a bowl and wash three or four times, until the water is clear. Do the same with the pigeon peas or mung beans. Once washed, leave to soak for 30 minutes.

Heat the oil and ghee in a large casserole with a lid over a medium heat. Add the bay leaves, cloves, cardamom and cinnamon to the heated oil. Stir gently, then add the cumin seeds and chilli, if using, and, once it starts crackling, add the onions. Cook for 3 minutes, then add the garlic and fry this mixture until it begins to brown.

Add the yellow split lentils and cook, stirring, for 4 minutes, roasting the lentils. Add the chopped tomatoes, turmeric and half the ginger. Mix well and cook for a further 3 minutes. Drain the pigeon peas or mung beans and add to the pan with 400ml water. Cover and simmer for 15 minutes.

Drain the rice and red lentils, and add to the mixture. Stir and add another 600ml water. Bring to the boil, then reduce the heat to a simmer, cover and simmer for 25 minutes.

Add the remaining ginger, the petit pois, sugar, asafoetida and a teaspoon of salt, then cover and simmer for a further 7 minutes. Check that the lentils and mung beans are tender before serving.

\\\\\ TIP /////

Traditionally, khitchuri
is quite porridge-like, with a
soft consistency.

VEGAN
BLACK BEAN STEW

SERVES 4–6

PREP TIME: 20 MINS • COOK TIME: 1¼ HOURS

(WF • GF if served without bread) • DF • V • Ve

coconut oil

2 **onions**, diced

6 cloves of **garlic**, minced

1 tablespoon **minced fresh ginger**

1 **leek**, halved lengthwise, then sliced

½ **chilli**, seeded and finely chopped

2 tablespoons **chopped coriander stalks**

2 **green peppers**, seeded, and cut into large dice

2 **carrots**, sliced into half-moons

2 **sweet potatoes**, peeled and cut into 3cm chunks

2 **bay leaves**

a pinch of **ground cloves**

1 teaspoon **smoked paprika**

2 × 400g cans of **organic black beans**, with their liquid

1 × 400g can of **chopped tomatoes**

juice of 1 **orange**

TO SERVE:

a large handful of **fresh coriander leaves**, chopped

flatbreads, **corn** or **wheat tortillas** or **microwave rice**

Black beans are commonly used in Central and South American cooking. Although they are great with meat, they come into their own when used in vegetarian and vegan dishes, where their smoky creaminess can claim centre stage. (John actually prefers it with meat! But enjoys this too…)

Place a knob or splash of coconut oil into a large pan and set it over a low–medium heat. Add the onions, garlic, ginger, leeks, chilli and coriander stalks and sauté. Once the onions have softened, add the peppers, carrots, sweet potatoes, bay leaves and spices. Stir and cook for a couple of minutes. Add the black beans and tomatoes, bring to the boil, then turn the heat right down and simmer for 1 hour.

Stir in the orange juice, top with the coriander and serve with flatbreads, tortillas or rice.

\\\\ **TIP** ////

Any leftovers can be used as a filling for quesadillas (see page 28), or on top of jacket potatoes, with some grated cheese.

SPANISH CHICKEN

SERVES 4

PREP TIME: 20 MINS • COOK TIME: 1 HOUR

WF • GF • DF

2 large **red onions**, each cut into
6 wedges

1 bulb of **garlic**, cloves peeled
and smashed

zest and juice of 1 **organic
unwaxed orange**

250g **cherry tomatoes**

2 **red peppers**, seeded and cut into
large slices

8 skin-on, bone-in **chicken thighs**

400g **small new potatoes**, halved

1 teaspoon **sweet** or **hot smoked
paprika**

1 teaspoon **fennel seeds**

2 tablespoons **olive oil**

2 tablespoons **chopped fresh parsley**

sea salt and lots of **cracked black
pepper**

*This is a staple in the Vincent–Derham household. John would like to
dedicate this to Natasha and Eleanor. Just because.*

*Cooking with lemon is common, but we forget that orange works brilliantly
with meat – especially paired with smoky paprika and fennel seeds.*

Heat the oven to 180°C/350°F/gas mark 4.

Put everything apart from the parsley and half the orange juice into a roasting dish.
Season with salt and lots of black pepper and toss together to coat. Roast in the
preheated oven for 40–60 minutes, until the chicken thighs are cooked through, the
juices run clear and the meat is pulling from the bones. (Cover with foil if the dish
contents start to colour too much.)

Toss with the parsley and the remaining orange juice, to serve.

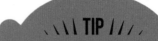

TIP

It can be hard to find unwaxed citrus
fruit, and even some organic fruit and veg is
coated with wax to help it last longer. However,
if you choose organic fruit, any wax used will be
natural rather than synthetic.

SMOKED HADDOCK GRATIN

SERVES 4
PREP TIME: 15 MINS • COOK TIME: 1 HOUR 10 MINS

a splash of **vegetable oil**

2 **leeks**, trimmed and finely sliced

a knob of **butter**

300ml **double cream**

150ml **whole milk**

a pinch of **freshly grated nutmeg**

a sprig of **fresh thyme**, leaves only

2 tablespoons **plain flour**

600g **Maris Piper potatoes**, cut into very
thin slices, ideally using a mandolin

350g **smoked haddock**, ideally
undyed, sliced into 1cm pieces

salt and **freshly ground black pepper**

green salad, to serve

A smoky, ramped-up one-pot twist on dauphinoise potatoes.

Heat the oven to 180°C/350°F/gas mark 4.

Pour a splash of oil into a heavy-based ovenproof pan (an ovenproof frying pan or wide, oven-safe casserole dish, about 25cm in diameter). Set over a low heat and add the leeks and a pinch of salt. Cook gently, stirring, to soften but not colour, for about 10 minutes, then scoop out the leeks, set aside, and add a knob of butter to the pan. When the butter has melted, swirl it around to coat the pan and remove from the heat.

In a jug, whisk together the cream, milk, nutmeg, thyme leaves and some black pepper. Remove 2 tablespoons of this mixture and whisk together with the flour until completely smooth. Pour back into the milk and cream mixture and mix thoroughly. (This will help to stop the cream splitting in the oven.)

Arrange one third of the sliced potatoes on the bottom of the buttered pan and top with half the smoked haddock and half the cooked leeks. Repeat, finishing with the final third of sliced potatoes. Press everything down, using your hands.

Finally, pour over the cream and milk mixture. It should just submerge the very top slices of potato – add a tiny splash more cream if necessary. Season generously with a little more nutmeg and some salt and pepper on top.

Slide the pan into the preheated oven and cook for 50–60 minutes. The gratin is ready when the top is golden brown and a sharp knife slides easily through the layers of potato. Serve with a crunchy green salad (we love fennel and parsley, dressed with lemon) to offset the gratin's smoky richness.

\\\ TIP ///

A layer of cooked spinach, chopped and very, very well squeezed out, wouldn't go amiss in the middle – just microwave an open bag of ready-washed leaves, cool, squeeze until almost completely dry, and add with the first layer of fish.

OVEN-BAKED RISOTTO

SERVES 4

PREP TIME: 15 MINS • COOK TIME: 35 MINS

WF · GF

3 tablespoons **butter**

150g **mixed mushrooms**, torn into small pieces

1 **onion**, finely diced

2 cloves of **garlic**, crushed

300g **risotto rice**

125ml **dry white wine**

1 litre good-quality hot **chicken** or **vegetable stock**

4 tablespoons **freshly grated Parmesan**, plus more to serve

salt and **freshly ground black pepper**

fresh parsley, chopped, to serve

Although we love the meditative process of stirring a stovetop risotto, this method means you can get on with something pressing – putting kids to bed/binge-watching Netflix – while the hard work is done for you. The texture is slightly softer than a traditional risotto, but it is still beautifully soothing.

Heat the oven to 180°C/350°F/gas mark 4.

Put a large ovenproof pan with a lid over a low–medium heat and add 2 tablespoons of the butter. When melted, add the mushrooms and cook, stirring, until beginning to turn golden. Remove half the mushrooms and set aside. Next, add the onions and sauté gently for 6 minutes, until they are just translucent. Add the garlic and cook for 1 minute, then add the rice and stir well to coat it in the butter. After a couple of minutes, add the wine and let bubble for 2 minutes longer. Next, add all the hot stock at once, season the mixture generously with salt and pepper and bring to a simmer. Scrape the bottom of the pan with a spoon to pick up any grains which have stuck to the base. Cover tightly with a lid and place in the preheated oven for 18 minutes.

Remove from the oven and taste to check that the rice is done to your liking. Add the remaining butter, the Parmesan and some more salt and pepper, tasting as you go. Add the remaining cooked mushrooms and stir; they will heat through in the hot risotto. Serve straight away, with extra Parmesan and some fresh parsley.

\\\\ TIP ////

See the risottos on pages 96–100 for more filling and topping ideas.

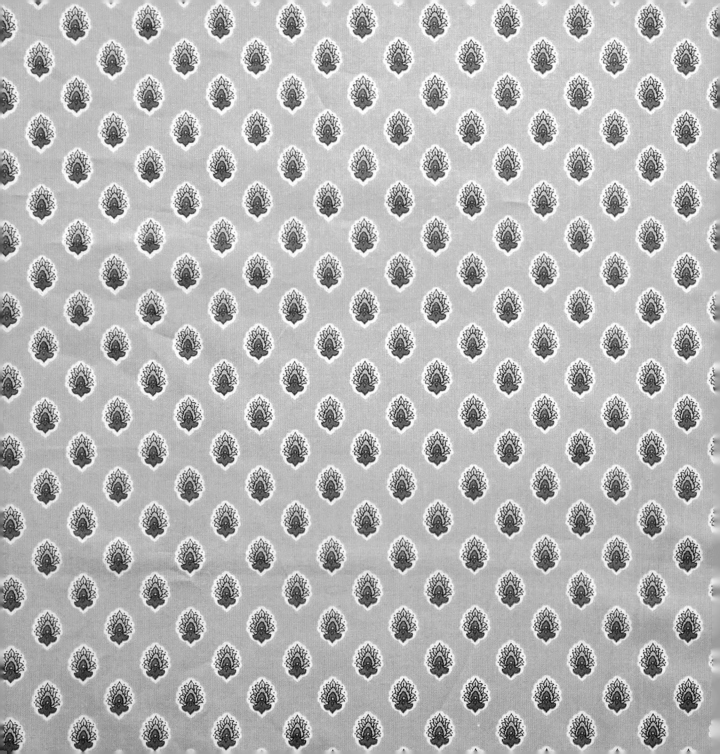

LOW
&
SLOW

IRISH STEW

SERVES 4

PREP TIME: 20 MINS • COOK TIME: 2 HOURS 20 MINS

WF · DF

1 tablespoon **flavourless oil**

600g **lamb shoulder**, trimmed of fat and
cut into chunks

2 **onions**, chopped into rough
1–2cm pieces

200g **carrots**, chopped into rough
1–2cm pieces

1 litre **lamb**, **chicken** or **vegetable stock**
or **hot water**

1 **bay leaf**

1 sprig of **fresh thyme**

75g **pearl barley**

650g **potatoes**, peeled and sliced
into 2cm chunks

200g **green cabbage** or **spring
greens**, shredded

salt and **freshly ground black pepper**

*Despite being incredibly simple, this comfortingly old-fashioned stew is
very tasty. You could use more meat, but the point of this thrifty dish is
to stretch an inexpensive cut much further than it might otherwise go.
We add cabbage to the pan at the end for a bit of sweet crunch.*

*PS: If you are making this for children it's a good time to teach them the
knock-knock joke…'Irish stew in the name of the Law.'*

Put a large casserole dish with a lid over a high heat and add the oil. When shimmering
hot, add the lamb. Brown it thoroughly all over, working in batches if necessary so
as not to crowd the pan and boil the meat. Return all the meat to the pan and add
the onions and carrots. Cook for a couple of minutes – you don't need to soften or
brown the onions – then add the water or stock, bay leaf, thyme and some salt and
pepper. Bring to a gentle simmer, then turn the heat right down so it's just bubbling,
cover and cook for an hour.

Add the pearl barley to the pan and cover again. Cook for a further 30 minutes.

Add the potatoes, pressing them into the broth to submerge them. Turn the heat up
slightly and uncover the pan, so that the broth can reduce a little. Cook for another
30 minutes, skimming off any scum or excess fat on the surface. By this point the
lamb should be meltingly tender and the potatoes and barley fully cooked. Add the
shredded cabbage to the broth and cook for 5 minutes, until tender.

Before serving, taste to check the seasoning. Serve in wide shallow bowls.

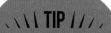

\ \ \ \ TIP / / / /

If you love root vegetables, swap
some of the potatoes for roughly
chopped turnips or swede, added
at the same time as the barley.

SPICY LAMB-STUFFED AUBERGINES

SERVES 2
PREP TIME: 20 MINS • COOK TIME: 1 HOUR

3–4 tablespoons **olive oil**

2 **aubergines**, untrimmed, cut in
   half lengthways

250g **20%-fat lamb mince**

1 **onion**, finely chopped

1 tablespoon **pine nuts**

1 tablespoon **tomato purée**

½ teaspoon **ground cumin**

1 large **tomato**, seeded and
   finely chopped

1 tablespoon **chopped fresh parsley**

1 tablespoon **chopped fresh dill**

salt and **freshly ground black pepper**

TO SERVE:

warm **flatbreads**, **pita** or **Turkish bread**

Greek- or **Turkish-style yoghurt**

This is a much simplified one-pot version of a Turkish favourite, karniyarik, which Rebecca discovered while working in Istanbul a few years ago.

Heat the oven to 200°C/400°F/gas mark 6.

Use a large, wide ovenproof pan with a lid (ours is 30cm wide). Set it over a medium heat and add 3 tablespoons of olive oil. With the cut sides facing upwards, slash three lines straight down the length of each aubergine half, without breaking the skin underneath. Place the aubergines, cut side down first, in the pan and brown them all over. Remove from the pan and season well with salt and pepper. Set aside.

Add the lamb to the same pan and brown it well too – do this in batches if necessary, so that the meat browns rather than stews. Return all the meat to the pan and add the onion. Cook, stirring, until the onion is just beginning to brown, around 10 minutes. Next add the pine nuts and toast for a minute or two, then add the tomato purée and cook, stirring, for a couple of minutes. Add the cumin and chopped fresh tomato, then 200ml hot water. Bring up to a gentle simmer and let bubble for 10 minutes. Add the chopped herbs, then taste and season as needed.

Return the aubergines to the pan and arrange them cut side up. Use a large spoon to scoop up the lamb mixture and pile it on top of the aubergines, dividing it equally between the 4 halves and pulling the slashes in each one apart slightly so that they open up during cooking.

Pour an extra 50ml hot water into the pan, cover with a lid and cook in the preheated oven for 20 minutes. Remove the lid, baste the aubergines and lamb with the pan juices and return to the oven for a further 10 minutes.

Remove from the oven and check that the aubergines are well cooked – they should be almost collapsing and soft all the way through. If they are not, cover the pan again (to protect the meat from burning) and return to the oven for 5 minutes.

Serve with warm bread to mop up the juices, and a dollop of thick yoghurt on the side.

FEIJOADA

SERVES 6–8

PREP TIME: 25 MINS, plus overnight soaking • COOK TIME: 3 HOURS 35 MINS

WF • GF (check sausage ingredients) • DF

a splash of **flavourless oil**

100g **smoked pancetta**, diced

500g **pork ribs**

3 **chorizo picante cooking sausages**, chopped

500g **pork shoulder**, trimmed of excess fat and cut into 5cm cubes

3 large **onions**, chopped

1 bulb of **garlic**, cloves separated and peeled

1 **fresh chilli**, seeded and chopped

1 large **tomato**, seeded and diced

2 **bay leaves**

¼ teaspoon **ground cloves**

juice of 1 **orange**

1 tablespoon **red wine vinegar**

250g **dried black beans**, soaked overnight, then drained

2 **sweet potatoes**, peeled and chopped into chunks

100g **kale**, chopped

salt and **freshly ground black pepper**

TOPPING:

2 handfuls **fresh coriander leaves**, finely chopped

2 handfuls **fresh parsley**, finely chopped

2 **spring onions**, finely chopped

zest of 1 **orange**

A meaty, spicy, low-and-slow stew from Brazil which is even better reheated. This makes a lot, but just pop any leftovers into the freezer. John and Katie had this at their wedding and John would like to thank his father-in-law (also called John), for spending the morning of the wedding making sure the caterers knew how to make it.

Put a large heavy-based saucepan with a lid over a medium heat. Add the oil and pancetta and fry until crisp. Remove the pancetta, leaving the oil in the pan.

Working in batches so as not to crowd the pan and stew the meat, sear the ribs, sausages and pork shoulder until browned all over. Season each batch with salt and pepper.

Remove the meat and set aside. Turn the heat to low and add the onions and garlic to the pan. Season with salt and pepper and fry, stirring, for 10 minutes or until soft. Return the meats to the pan and add everything else except the beans, sweet potatoes and kale. Cover with water, bring to a simmer and put the lid on the pan. After 2 hours, add the beans and simmer for 30 minutes. If any scum forms on the surface of the stew, skim it off.

Add the sweet potatoes for a final 30 minutes of cooking. Remove the lid and allow the liquid to reduce, if the stew seems very wet. By now, the meat should be falling apart tender and the beans should be soft and creamy.

Check that the beans and sweet potatoes are fully cooked, then, 5 minutes before you are ready to eat, add the kale.

Mix together the topping ingredients. Remove the pan from the heat and sprinkle the topping over the stew before serving.

\\\\ **TIP** ////

You can make this with cooked black
beans if you prefer. You will need
2 × 400g cans, which will give you
about 500g of beans once drained.
Add them at the same time as the
sweet potatoes. As they won't absorb
liquid like dried beans, you will need to
remove the lid to reduce the sauce.

LAMB SHANK TAGINE

SERVES 4
PREP TIME: 20 MINS • COOK TIME: 2 HOURS 40 MINS
WF • GF (if served without bread) • DF

1 tablespoon **flavourless oil**

4 **lamb shanks**, approx. 400g each

2 large **onions**, finely diced

1 **aubergine**, cut into cubes

2cm piece of **fresh ginger**,
  peeled and finely grated

3 cloves of **garlic**, crushed

½ teaspoon **ground cinnamon**

2 teaspoons **paprika**

1 teaspoon **ground turmeric**

1 × 400g can of **chopped tomatoes**

generous pinch of **saffron threads**

600ml hot **lamb**, **chicken** or
  vegetable stock (or enough to cover
  the meat)

15 **dried apricots**, halved

5 heaped tablespoons **flaked almonds**

1 **preserved lemon**, flesh scraped out
  and peel very finely diced

freshly ground black pepper

TO SERVE:

fresh **coriander** or **parsley**

hunks of warm **fresh bread**, ideally
  Moroccan **khobz**

In a Moroccan home, a proper tagine would never be served with couscous – for some reason, it was a habit adopted by tourists which has spread worldwide. Usually tagines are served with bread, often khobz, a round white loaf. We break with tradition in another way, as a real tagine should be made in a special, rather beautiful earthenware tagine pot. Given that, feel free to serve this heretical version of the stew with couscous.

This freezes well and is one of those dishes which is almost better the next day.

Heat the oven to 160°C/325°F/gas mark 3.

Place a large ovenproof pan (one big enough for all the meat) with a lid over a high heat. Add the oil and, when shimmering, add the meat and brown each shank all over. Remove and set aside, then turn the heat down to medium and add the onions. Sauté until golden, about 8 minutes. Then add the aubergine and cook for a further 5 minutes. Add the ginger and garlic and cook for 1 minute, stirring. Return the meat to the pan. Add the ground spices with a pinch of black pepper and stir, then add the tomatoes, saffron, stock, dried apricots and almonds. The liquid should almost cover the meat.

Bring to a simmer, then cover with a lid and place in the preheated oven for 1½ hours, topping up the liquid with a little water every now and then, if necessary. Remove from the oven. The meat should be very tender and beginning to fall away from the bones – if not, return it to the oven for another 15–30 minutes.

Remove the lid from the pan. If there is a lot of fat on top of the sauce, skim it off. Add the preserved lemon peel. Stir well, turn the lamb shanks over, then spoon some of the sauce over the meat. Return to the oven for 15 minutes, to reduce the sauce slightly.

Serve with the fresh herbs on top and some warm bread for scooping up the sauce.

\\\ TIP ///

In season, swap the dried apricots for slices of uncooked quince, added with the liquid.

INDIAN BAKED CHICKEN & RICE

SERVES 4

PREP TIME: 30 MINS, plus at least 30 mins marinating • COOK TIME: 1 HOUR 10 MINS, plus 10 mins standing

WF · GF

CHICKEN:

½ teaspoon **fennel seeds**

1 teaspoon **coriander seeds**

5 heaped tablespoons **full-fat yoghurt**

1½ teaspoons **garam masala**

2 cloves of **garlic**, crushed

3cm piece of **fresh ginger**, peeled and grated

1 teaspoon **ground turmeric**

a small handful of **fresh coriander leaves** and **stalks**, roughly chopped

15 **fresh mint leaves**

½ teaspoon **chilli flakes**

¼ teaspoon **freshly ground black pepper**

½ teaspoon **fine salt**

4–8 boneless **chicken thighs**, depending on their size and your hunger

RICE:

a splash of **flavourless oil**

3 **onions**, finely sliced

250g **basmati rice**, soaked and drained

6 **cardamom pods**

8 **curry leaves**

1 × 400g can of **chickpeas**, drained and rinsed

This is halfway between an Indian pulao and a biryani, and steals and blends the spicing from both.

RAITA:

6 tablespoons **full-fat thick plain** or **Greek-style yoghurt**

a pinch of **ground cumin**

a pinch of **salt**

1 **tomato**, seeded and finely diced

6cm **chunk of cucumber**, finely diced

1 tablespoon very finely diced **onion**

2 tablespoons **finely chopped fresh coriander**

First make the marinade: using a pestle and mortar, roughly grind the fennel seeds and coriander seeds. Place this mixture and everything else apart from the chicken into a blender and blitz to form a paste. Pour the marinade over the chicken, rub it in, cover, place in the fridge and leave to marinate for at least 30 minutes (but several hours or overnight is better).

When ready to cook, set a large wide pan with a lid over a low heat. Add the oil and, when hot, add the onions. Cook gently, until deep brown but not burnt, around 20–25 minutes, stirring often. Remove half the onions and set aside.

Push the remaining onions to one side of the pan. Add the marinated chicken, leaving any leftover marinade in the bowl for later. Turn the heat to medium and sauté gently for 10 minutes.

Next, drain the soaked rice and add it to the pan along with the cardamom pods and curry leaves. Stir everything together and let the rice toast in the yoghurty oil in the pan for a couple of minutes. Add a couple of tablespoons of hot water to the remaining marinade and mix, to temper the yoghurt to the heat of the pan. Then pour into the pan along with 350ml hot water and the drained chickpeas. Bring up to a simmer, then turn the heat down, cover tightly and cook for 30 minutes.

Remove the lid and check to see if the chicken is cooked by piercing one of the thighs at the thickest part – the juices should run clear. If not, return to the heat, with the lid on, for another 5 minutes.

Remove from the heat and leave to stand with the lid partly on, for 10 minutes, before serving. Meanwhile, make the raita by simply mixing together all the ingredients.

Eat with the reserved caramelized onions scattered on top, with dollops of the raita on the side, avoiding the cardamom pods and curry leaves.

\\\\ TIP ////

Don't rush cooking the onions, as they will easily burn and be bitter.

BEEF & BUTTERNUT TAGINE

SERVES 6

PREP TIME: 20 MINS • COOK TIME: 2¾ HOURS

(WF • GF if served without bread) • DF

2 tablespoons **olive oil**

2 large **onions**, sliced

8 cloves of **garlic**, crushed

2 tablespoons **finely chopped
   fresh coriander stalks**

a pinch of **saffron threads**

1 teaspoon **ground ginger**

1 teaspoon **ground cinnamon**

1 teaspoon **paprika**

1 teaspoon **ground turmeric**

½ teaspoon **ground cumin**

600g **stewing beef**, cut into chunks

2 **preserved lemons**, flesh scraped out
   and peel finely diced

10 **dried apricots**, roughly chopped

600ml **stock** or **water**

1 **butternut squash**, peeled and
   cut into large chunks

juice of ½ **lemon**

warm **bread**, to serve

Tender beef and sweet, slow-cooked butternut. Like the tagines on pages 168 and 184, this wouldn't be served with couscous in North Africa. (You should, of course, if you want to.)

Set a large heavy-based saucepan with a lid over a medium heat. Add the olive oil and sliced onions and fry for 10 minutes, until beginning to brown, then add the garlic, coriander stalks and spices and cook, stirring, for 1 minute. Next, add the beef and stir to coat with the onion and spice mix. After 2 minutes, add the preserved lemon peel, dried apricots and stock or water.

Put on a tight-fitting lid and simmer gently for 1½ hours. Add the squash and cook with the lid on for a further hour.

During cooking, you may need to add some more water if the sauce becomes too dry, or if there isn't enough stock to cover the squash. If there is too much liquid at the end of cooking, simmer with the lid off to reduce; the end result should be thick enough to coat the back of a spoon.

When you think the tagine is done, taste to check that the beef is absolutely tender. Depending on the stock, you may need to add a little salt. Stir in the lemon juice before serving with warm bread.

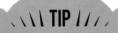

TIP

This is a freezer favourite of ours. If cooking for 4, freeze the remaining 2 portions for a rainy day.

BEEF MASSAMAN CURRY

SERVES 4–6

PREP TIME: 25 MINS • COOK TIME: 2¾ HOURS

WF · GF · DF

CURRY PASTE:

5 **dried red chillies**

50g roasted **unsalted peanuts**

50g **desiccated coconut**

1 tablespoon **ground coriander**

1 teaspoon **ground cumin**

¼ teaspoon **ground cloves**

¼ teaspoon **freshly grated nutmeg**

3 **shallots**, peeled and roughly chopped

1 bulb of **garlic**, cloves peeled

6cm piece of **galangal**, roughly chopped

3 **lemongrass stalks**, trimmed and roughly chopped

a handful of **fresh coriander stalks**

CURRY:

2 tablespoons **coconut oil**

800ml **coconut cream**

3cm piece of **cassia bark**

2 **black cardamom pods**

4 **green cardamom pods**

3 **bay leaves**

2–4 tablespoons **fish sauce**, to taste

2–3 tablespoons **palm** or **coconut sugar**, to taste

Although usually served with rice, this Thai one-pot doesn't necessarily need it, as the recipe already contains new potatoes, cooked in the mild coconut curry.

(Curry continued...)

1–3 tablespoons **tamarind paste**, to taste

¼ teaspoon **freshly ground black pepper**

600g **stewing beef**, cut into chunks

300g **new potatoes**, halved

300g **green vegetables (kale, green beans, tenderstem broccoli** or a mixture) (optional)

microwave rice, to serve (optional)

Set a large pan, big enough for all the ingredients, over a medium heat. To make the curry paste, toast the chillies, peanuts, coconut and spices in the hot dry pan for a couple of minutes, stirring, until fragrant. Tip this mixture into a food processor with the shallots, garlic, galangal, lemongrass and coriander stalks, and blend to form a paste. Add a little water to loosen, if needed.

Melt the coconut oil in the hot pan, turn the heat to low, and add the paste. Cook it gently for 5 minutes, then add 200ml water along with the rest of the curry ingredients except the beef, potatoes and green vegetables. Bring to a simmer, then taste to see if you would like to add more fish sauce, sugar or tamarind paste – the curry should be a good balance of salty, sweet and sour.

Add the beef. Stir, then simmer, covered, for 1½ hours, stirring occasionally. Add the potatoes and cook for a further hour. The curry is ready when the beef is absolutely tender. If using, add the green vegetables for the last 5 minutes of the cooking time. Serve with rice, if liked.

\\\\ TIP ////

Instead of beef, you could use boneless chicken, which would need about 12–15 minutes cooking time, or until cooked through.

SUPER SIMPLE
SUNDAY ROAST CHICKEN

SERVES 4

PREP TIME: 25 MINS • COOK TIME: 1 HOUR 55 MINS

- -

600g **potatoes** (you can use either **floury potatoes**, peeled and cut into chunks, or whole **new potatoes**)

300g **carrots**, cut into large chunks

200g **parsnips**, cut into large chunks

2 sprigs of **fresh rosemary**

1 bulb of **garlic**, cut in half across the middle

5 tablespoons **olive oil**

1.5kg whole **chicken**

5 sprigs of **fresh thyme**

1 tablespoon **butter** (optional)

300g **seasonal hardy green vegetables** (**asparagus**, **broccoli** or **Brussels sprouts**)

150ml **dry white wine**

1 tablespoon **plain flour**

salt and **freshly ground black pepper**

Is there anything better than a weekend roast? Time stands still, and for a short while you know everything is gonna be OK.

- -

Heat the oven to 200°C/400°F/gas mark 6. Use a large metal baking dish with sides.

Arrange the potatoes, carrots, parsnips, rosemary and half the split bulb of garlic in the dish in a single layer. Pour over 3 tablespoons of the oil, and season well with salt and pepper. Toss.

Nestle the chicken into the vegetables. Tuck the remaining half bulb of garlic and all the thyme into the cavity, then season generously all over and rub the remaining oil into the skin. Gently lift the skin away from the breast meat and push the butter, if using, under it.

Place in the preheated oven and cook for 30 minutes, then turn the heat down to 180°C/350°F/gas mark 4 and cook for a further 1 hour.

Remove the tray from the oven. Check the chicken is cooked by piercing one of the thighs at the thickest point – the juices should run clear. Remove the chicken and set aside, wrapped loosely in foil, somewhere warm to rest.

Add the green vegetables to the pan and return it to the oven for 15 minutes. Remove everything from the pan and keep warm while you make the gravy.

Set the baking dish over a medium heat on the hob. Add the wine and deglaze the pan, scraping up any burnt bits as the liquid bubbles. Add a little salt and pepper, then remove a couple of tablespoons of the liquid and blend with the flour to form a smooth, loose paste. Return this mixture to the pan and cook, stirring, adding just enough hot water to make a gravy.

Serve the rested chicken with the warm vegetables and the gravy.

\\\\ TIP ////

It's hard to beat an old-school roast but we love spicing things up. Rub your chicken with lemony ground sumac, cumin and coriander, switch the potatoes for squash and replace the gravy with garlicky yoghurt.

ROASTED SQUASH STUFFED WITH FREEKEH & FETA

SERVES 4

PREP TIME: 15 MINS • COOK TIME: 1 HOUR

V

2 small **butternut squash** (about 1kg)

4 tablespoons **olive oil**

1 teaspoon **ground cumin**

½ teaspoon **ground coriander**

1 **red pepper**, seeded and diced

1 **onion**, diced

1 **courgette**, diced (remove and discard any seedy bits)

150g **ready-cooked freekeh**

150g **feta**, crumbled into chunks

1 tablespoon **finely chopped fresh chives**

½ teaspoon crumbled **chilli flakes**, or more to taste

1 tablespoon **pumpkin seeds**

salt and **freshly ground black pepper**

TO SERVE:

2 tablespoons **roughly chopped fresh coriander**

extra virgin olive oil

Freekeh is toasted green wheat with a nutty, smoky flavour. It is sold both dried and ready-cooked, and is widely available.

Heat the oven to 200°C/400°F/gas mark 6.

Halve the squash and use a spoon to scoop out the seeds and stringy flesh. Drizzle 2 tablespoons of the oil over the squash and season with salt and pepper; use your hands to rub the oil all over the cut sides of the flesh.

Put the squash into a large metal baking dish, flesh side down, and place in the hot oven. Cook for 30 minutes, then remove from the oven. Mix the ground cumin and coriander with another tablespoon of oil; turn the squash cut side up and drizzle this mixture over.

Toss the diced vegetables in the remaining oil with some more salt and pepper. Add to the baking dish, arranging them in a single layer around the squash. Return to the oven for a further 20 minutes.

Remove from the oven and spoon out the diced cooked vegetables. Put them into a bowl with the freekeh, feta, chives and chilli flakes and stir to combine. Pile this mixture into the hollow of each squash – don't worry if some falls out into the dish. Top each half with a sprinkle of pumpkin seeds. Return to the oven for 8 minutes, to heat through the freekeh, pop the seeds and warm the cheese.

Top with the fresh coriander and a restrained drizzle of extra virgin olive oil just before serving.

SLOW-COOKED LAMB

SERVES 4

PREP TIME: 20 MINS · COOK TIME: 3 HOURS 40 MINS

WF · GF · DF

1kg **shoulder of lamb**, bone in

1 **onion**, cut into 8 wedges

2 tablespoons **olive oil**

2 sprigs of **fresh rosemary**,
broken into 3 or 4 pieces

4 cloves of **garlic**, sliced lengthwise
into quarters

250ml good-quality **chicken** or
vegetable stock

20 **small ripe cherry tomatoes**, halved

250g **ready-cooked Puy lentils**

10 **black olives**, pitted and torn into
2 or 3 pieces

200g **whole leaf spinach**

salt and **freshly ground black pepper**

For this lamb dish, first slow-cook the meat, then use the same tin and the lamb's roasting juices to cook everything else – wilted spinach, roasted tomatoes and nutty, firm little Puy lentils.

Heat the oven to 200°C/400°F/gas mark 6.

Toss the lamb and onion wedges in the oil, salt and pepper, then place in a large roasting dish. Use a sharp knife to make small holes all over the meat, then poke the rosemary pieces and garlic slivers into the holes.

Place in the preheated oven and cook for 20 minutes.

Remove from the oven and turn the heat down to 140°C/275°F/gas mark 1. Add the stock to the roasting dish, then cover tightly with foil and return it to the oven. Roast for 2½–3 hours, until the meat is completely tender.

Remove from the oven and strain the liquid into a jug to reduce the fat (take the lamb out for a moment if it's easier), leaving the onion and garlic behind. Turn the heat back up to 200°C/400°F/gas mark 6. Add the halved tomatoes to the dish with the lamb, plus a couple of spoonfuls of the reserved liquid, and return it to the oven for 15 minutes.

Now, remove the lamb and set it aside, wrapped in foil, somewhere warm to rest.

Add the lentils, torn olives and spinach to the pan, plus 3 more spoonfuls of the reserved liquid. Stir gently and return to the oven for 5 minutes. Return the rested lamb to the dish and serve at the table.

The meat will be so tender that it will naturally shred as you cut into it. Serve a tangle of the meat on top of the lentils and spinach, with the roasted tomatoes and roasting juices.

TIP

Swap the lentils for chickpeas, haricot or cannellini beans; add artichoke hearts instead of olives.

STEAK & ALE STEW
WITH HERBY DUMPLINGS

SERVES 4

PREP TIME: 25 MINS · COOK TIME: 4 HOURS

DF

· ·

2 tablespoons **flavourless oil**

500g **stewing steak**, cut into chunks

1 tablespoon **plain flour**

1 **onion**, diced

1 medium **carrot**, diced

1 small **leek**, finely sliced

1 stick of **celery**, diced

1 teaspoon **tomato purée**

500ml **golden ale**

100ml **beef stock**

1 **bay leaf**

2 sprigs of **fresh thyme**

a dash of **Worcestershire sauce**
    (optional)

DUMPLINGS:

200g **plain flour**

a pinch of **fine salt**

1½ teaspoons **baking powder**

100g **shredded suet** (**beef** or **vegetable**)

2 tablespoons **finely chopped**
    fresh parsley

2 tablespoons **finely chopped**
    fresh chives

125ml **cold water**, or enough to make
    a soft dough

After a slow cook, top this stew with light, herby little dumplings – they will puff up as they simmer while becoming golden and crunchy on top.

· ·

Put a wide casserole dish with a lid over a high heat and add half the oil. Dust the steak pieces with the flour and, when the oil is hot, add them to the pan and brown thoroughly (do this in batches if necessary, to stop the meat boiling in its own liquid). Remove and set aside, then turn the heat to medium and add the other tablespoon of oil and the vegetables. Sauté, stirring, until they begin to soften, about 10 minutes. Add the tomato purée and cook for 2 minutes, stirring.

Return the meat to the casserole and add the ale and the stock, along with the bay leaf, thyme and Worcestershire sauce, if using. Bring to a simmer, then cover with a lid and cook for 3 hours, or until the meat is so tender that it is falling apart.

Heat the oven to 180°C/350°F/gas mark 4.

To make the dumplings, mix the flour, salt, baking powder, suet and herbs together in a bowl. Slowly mix in the water, stopping as soon as a soft dough forms. Divide the mixture into 16 equally-sized pieces and gently roll into small balls.

Remove the lid from the casserole. If the stew seems at all dry, add a little hot water before adding the dumplings, as it will reduce considerably in the oven. Dot the stew with the dumplings, which should rest with their bottoms in the liquid. Slide the pan into the oven and cook with the lid off for 30 minutes, or until the dumplings have puffed up slightly and are golden on top.

Remove the bay leaf and thyme sprigs before serving.

\\\\ TIP ////

If you prefer, you can cook the stew in
the oven at 160°C/325°F/gas mark 3 for
3 hours, with the lid on, rather than
on the hob, once all the liquid has
been added.

VEGETABLE TAGINE

SERVES 4

PREP TIME: 20 MINS • COOK TIME: 1 HOUR 5 MINS

(WF • GF if served without bread or couscous) • DF • V • Ve

4 tablespoons **olive oil**

250g **cauliflower**, broken into small florets

1 small **aubergine**, cut into 2cm chunks

1 large **onion**, cut into wedges

1 small **butternut squash**, peeled and cut into 2cm chunks

1 **red pepper**, seeded and cut into 2cm chunks

1 **head of fennel**, trimmed and cut into 2cm chunks

1 teaspoon **ground coriander**

1 teaspoon **ground cumin**

1 teaspoon **ground turmeric**

1 × 3cm piece of **fresh ginger**, peeled and grated

1 × 400g can of **chopped tomatoes**

1 × 400g can of **chickpeas**, drained and rinsed

400ml **vegetable stock**

3 cloves of **garlic**, crushed

1 tablespoon **harissa paste**

generous pinch of **saffron threads**

3 tablespoons **raisins** (optional)

2 tablespoons **flaked almonds** or **pine nuts**

salt and **freshly ground black pepper**

warm **crusty white bread**, to serve

You have probably worked out by now that, as with the meaty tagines on pages 168 and 172, this shouldn't really be served with couscous – it's not how they do it in Morocco, where it's served with crusty bread called khobz. But we are starting to feel like food fascists, so what the hell, have it with couscous or chips.

Heat the oven to 200°C/400°F/gas mark 6.

Pour the oil into a large metal baking dish with high sides (if you don't have a big one, you may need to use two). Add the cauliflower, aubergine, onion, squash, red pepper and fennel and toss to cover with the oil. Spread out so the vegetable pieces lie more or less in a single layer. Place in the preheated oven and roast for 15 minutes.

Mix together the coriander, cumin, turmeric and a big pinch of salt, then sprinkle over the hot vegetables. Toss again to coat and return to the oven for a further 15 minutes.

Remove the tray from the oven and add the ginger, tomatoes, chickpeas, stock, garlic, harissa paste, saffron, raisins, if using, and lots of black pepper. Return to the oven and cook for 30 minutes, checking the liquid levels every now and then, and adding a little hot water if necessary. (This tagine should be neither dry nor thick.) Finally, scatter the almonds or pine nuts over the top and return to the oven for 5 minutes, or until toasted and golden, checking every couple of minutes, as the nuts can quickly burn.

Serve with warm, crusty white bread.

\\\\ TIP ////

When pouring in the stock, try adding a few chopped black olives, some diced preserved lemon peel, apricots instead of raisins, or swapping the squash for sweet potato. This is also good as a side to grilled fish, roast chicken, or spiced, slow-cooked lamb.

SIMPLE
SUPPERS

SPICED FISH & COUSCOUS

SERVES 4

PREP TIME: 20 MINS, plus 10 mins standing • COOK TIME: 20 MINS

DF

- -

400g **dried couscous**

3 tablespoons **finely chopped**
fresh chives

2 tablespoons **harissa paste**

3 tablespoons **olive oil**

4–6 heaped tablespoons
ready-made chermoula paste

4 boneless, skinless **firm white**
fish fillets (hake works well, or **cod,**
haddock or **pollock)**

70g **pitted dried black olives,**
roughly chopped

250g **cherry tomatoes,**
at room temperature

3 tablespoons **roughly chopped**
fresh parsley

2 teaspoons good-quality
extra virgin olive oil

salt and **freshly ground black pepper**

This includes North African spices and uses a French technique, 'en papillote', which means to cook something tightly wrapped in paper. Chermoula is a green North African spice paste, widely available in supermarkets, made with preserved lemons, coriander and parsley.

- -

Heat the oven to 200°C/400°F/gas mark 6.

Place the couscous and 400ml boiling water in a large bowl and immediately cover with clingfilm. Leave for 10 minutes, then remove the clingfilm, fluff up the couscous with a fork and allow to cool slightly.

Mix together the chives, harissa paste, olive oil and a pinch of salt, then use this mixture to dress the couscous. Stir thoroughly to coat each grain.

Divide the spiced couscous equally between 4 large sheets of baking paper, each around 45cm long.

Rub the chermoula paste all over the fish fillets, then place them on top of the couscous. Scatter over the chopped olives. Season everything with black pepper.

Pull the long sides of the paper up so they meet above the fish. Fold and crimp the paper edges together, working downwards until you meet the fish. Do the same with the paper at either end of the parcel, to prevent the parcels opening up. They should be snug around the filling, with no gaps for steam to escape.

Place in the preheated oven on a baking tray and bake for 15–20 minutes – for thin fillets bake for the lesser amount of time; chunky, meatier fillets will need longer.

Meanwhile, make the tomato salad: quarter the tomatoes, then mix them with the parsley, a pinch of salt and the extra virgin olive oil.

Place each parcel on a plate and let everyone open them at the table so that the fragrant steam escapes. Serve the tomato salad alongside.

GOCHUJANG CHICKEN WITH SESAME SLAW

SERVES 4

PREP TIME: 20 MINS • COOK TIME: 40 MINS, plus 10 mins resting

WF • GF (check soy sauce ingredients) • DF

2 tablespoons **soy sauce**

2 tablespoons **gochujang chilli paste**

2 cloves of **garlic**, crushed to a paste

2 tablespoons **maple syrup**

4 teaspoons **vegetable oil**

1 teaspoon **finely grated fresh ginger**

4 whole **chicken legs**

salt and **freshly ground black pepper**

toasted sesame seeds, to serve

SLAW:

1 large **carrot**, peeled and sliced into thin julienne pieces

2 **spring onions**, finely chopped

1 heaped tablespoon **fresh chilli**, seeded and very finely chopped

300g **cabbage**, shredded (**sweetheart** or **white cabbage** works best)

10 **radishes**, sliced into thin julienne pieces

200g **cucumber**, seeded and sliced into thin julienne pieces

2 tablespoons **fish sauce**

juice of ½ **lime**

4 teaspoons **rice vinegar**

Gochujang is a spicy Korean chilli paste. Available in larger supermarkets and South East Asian food stores, it is addictively good with fish, stirred into sauces or as part of noodle dishes.

(Slaw continued...)

3cm piece of **fresh ginger**, peeled and grated

3 tablespoons **sesame** or **vegetable oil**

1 tablespoon **honey** or **maple syrup**

1 tablespoon **toasted sesame seeds**

salt

Heat the oven to 200°C/400°F/gas mark 6.

Mix together the soy sauce, gochujang chilli paste, garlic, maple syrup, oil and ginger with some salt and pepper. Use 2 tablespoons of the sauce to glaze the chicken legs, spreading it evenly all over the skin and meat.

Place the chicken in the preheated oven and roast for 40 minutes, basting it once halfway through cooking.

Meanwhile, make the slaw: prepare all the vegetables, then make the dressing. Whisk together the fish sauce, lime juice, rice vinegar, ginger, oil, honey or maple syrup and a generous pinch of salt. Taste – it should be tangy but sweet, with a rich hit of umami. Add the sauce to the vegetables, stir and add the sesame seeds.

When the chicken is cooked (check the juices are running clear and the meat is pulling easily away from the bones), the skin will be dark and crisp. Remove from the oven and rest the meat somewhere warm for 10 minutes.

Sprinkle the chicken with a pinch of toasted sesame seeds, and serve with the slaw and the remaining gochujang sauce on the side.

TIP

This slaw also goes well with the sea bass with sticky aubergine & chilli on page 34.

PEA & POTATO CURRY

SERVES 4

PREP TIME: 10 MINS • COOK TIME: 40 MINS

(WF • GF if served without flatbreads) • (DF • Ve if served without dairy yogurt) • V

. . . .

1 tablespoon **vegetable oil**

10 **cardamom pods**

1 teaspoon **cumin seeds**

2 teaspoons **mustard seeds**

1 teaspoon **fennel seeds**

1 teaspoon **ground turmeric**

1 teaspoon **garam masala**

a pinch of **cayenne**

2 **onions**, grated

3 cloves of **garlic**, crushed

3cm piece of **fresh ginger**, peeled
    and grated

15 **dried curry leaves**

150g **cherry tomatoes**, halved

15 sprigs of **fresh coriander**,
    leaves picked, stalks retained and
    finely chopped

550g **small waxy potatoes**, halved

250g **fresh** or **frozen peas**

salt and **freshly ground black pepper**

TO SERVE:

flatbreads

yoghurt

spicy pickles

A gently spiced meal-in-a-bowl.

. . . .

Place a large saucepan over a medium heat. Add the oil and, when hot, the cardamom pods, cumin seeds, mustard seeds, fennel seeds, turmeric, garam masala, cayenne and a generous pinch of salt. Let sizzle for just a minute or two, then add the onions, garlic and ginger. Cook, stirring, for 5 minutes, then add the curry leaves, cherry tomatoes, coriander stalks and some black pepper. Cook for another 5 minutes, until the tomatoes begin to soften and collapse.

Next, add the potatoes with 450ml boiling water and bring up to a simmer. Let it bubble for 15 minutes, without a lid, stirring every now and then. When the potatoes are tender, add the peas and bring back to a simmer for a final 5 minutes. Garnish with the coriander leaves.

Serve with flatbreads, yoghurt and spicy pickles.

\\\\ TIP ////

This curry stands up well to being reheated, so is perfect for grown-up lunchboxes.

EASY CHEESY LASAGNE

SERVES 4

PREP TIME: 25 MINS · COOK TIME: 40 MINS, plus 5 mins standing

V

. . . .

250g **ricotta cheese**

150g **soft, mild, rindless goats' cheese**

a generous pinch of freshly grated **nutmeg**

150g **frozen chopped spinach**, defrosted and excess liquid squeezed out (pour boiling water over to speed this up if necessary) (optional)

1 **egg**

500ml **passata**

1 teaspoon **olive oil**, plus more for greasing

1 clove of **garlic**, crushed

approx. 15 **fresh basil leaves**, from 1 bushy sprig, torn

1 ball of **mozzarella**, ripped into bite-sized pieces

150g **ready-roasted aubergines**, **peppers** and/or **courgettes**, from a jar (optional)

50g **grated firm mozzarella**

6–9 sheets (approx.) **fresh egg lasagne**

salt and **freshly ground black pepper**

Unlike a meat and béchamel lasagne, you don't need to make the sauces for this one on the hob – just stir them up, layer and bake.

The essential parts of this recipe are the cheeses, pasta and tomato sauce. So, if you don't have frozen spinach, you can easily leave it out, and the roasted vegetables are not crucial either.

. . . .

Heat the oven to 190°C/375°F/gas mark 5.

In one bowl, mix together the ricotta, goats' cheese, nutmeg and squeezed-out spinach, if using, with a pinch of salt and black pepper. Taste, add more seasoning if necessary, then stir in the egg. In another bowl, mix together the passata, teaspoon of olive oil, garlic and the basil leaves, then taste and add a little pepper, if needed.

Grease a medium-sized ceramic baking dish. Cover the base with a very thin layer of tomato sauce, then cover with 2 or 3 sheets of lasagne. Spread one third of the ricotta cheese mixture over the pasta. Gently spread one third of the tomato sauce over the top.

If using, arrange the ready-roasted vegetables on top of the sauce and cover with another 2 or 3 sheets of lasagne. Add another third of the ricotta mixture, then another third of the tomato sauce. Scatter half the torn mozzarella on top of the sauce, then cover with 2 or 3 sheets of lasagne.

Spread the rest of the ricotta over the pasta, then the rest of the tomato sauce. Finally scatter the remaining half of the torn mozzarella evenly over the lasagne and finish with a layer of grated mozzarella. Season with lots of black pepper.

Bake in the preheated oven for 35–40 minutes, until bubbling and deep golden brown on top. Leave to stand and settle for 5 minutes before serving.

\\\\ TIP ////
Add a layer of ham, cooked sausage or bacon, or cooked mushrooms, instead of, or as well as, the vegetables.

PEA & RICOTTA HOTCAKE

SERVES 2 as a main course or 4 as part of a light meal
PREP TIME: 10 MINS • COOK TIME: 18 MINS

V

2 tablespoons **pumpkin seeds**

150g **frozen peas**, defrosted
(cover with boiling water to speed this
up if necessary)

150g **ricotta**

1 **spring onion**, finely chopped

1 tablespoon **finely chopped fresh mint**

2 **eggs**, separated

200ml **milk**

125g **flour**

1½ teaspoons **baking powder**

1 teaspoon **vegetable oil**

salt and **freshly ground black pepper**

TO SERVE:

1 teaspoon **lemon juice**

1 tablespoon **extra virgin olive oil**

a handful of **pea shoots**

10 whole **fresh mint leaves**

> ＼＼＼ **TIP** ／／／
>
> With all batters, for anything
> from pancakes to sponge,
> always mix liquid and dry
> ingredients as little as possible,
> as over-mixing will make the
> end results chewy and tough.

Hotcakes are like big, deep but very light American pancakes. Rebecca discovered them while working in Melbourne, where they are served at Top Paddock restaurant, covered in a riot of flowers and fruit. This one is savoury, studded with ricotta and accompanied by a herby little salad.

For this dish, use a small frying pan which can go under the grill. Place the pan over a medium heat. When hot, add the pumpkin seeds and toast briefly, just until they begin to pop. Remove the seeds from the pan and set aside.

Mash the peas roughly with a fork and place in a large bowl. Add the ricotta, spring onion and chopped mint. Whisk the egg yolks and milk together and add to the peas. Sift the flour into the pea mixture and add the baking powder, a generous pinch of salt and some pepper. Whisk the egg whites until foaming and bubbly, then add to the peas. Stir briefly. Stop when just combined – you want little chunks of cheese to remain.

Heat the grill to medium. Pour the vegetable oil into the pan and place it over a medium–low heat. When hot, pour in the batter. Cook for 3 or 4 minutes, then use a spatula to gently check the bottom of the hotcake – it should be browning nicely; adjust the heat as necessary. Once little bubbles start to appear on the surface of the hotcake, slide the pan under the preheated grill, making sure there is at least 10cm between the heat source and the top of the batter. Cook until the surface is a light golden colour.

Remove from the grill and use a sharp knife or skewer to check that the batter is set all the way through.

While the hotcake is cooking, whisk the lemon juice and extra virgin olive oil together with a pinch of salt. Use this to dress the pea shoots and mint leaves.

To serve, turn the hotcake out on to a serving plate. Serve warm, with the pea shoot salad and puffed seeds scattered over.

BAKED LAMB KOFTA WITH ROASTED VEGETABLES

SERVES 4

PREP TIME: 20 MINS • COOK TIME: 35 MINS

500g **lamb mince** (at least 20% fat)

1 **onion**, grated

2 cloves of **garlic**, crushed

½ teaspoon **chilli flakes**

½ teaspoon **ground cumin**

½ teaspoon **ground coriander**

a pinch of **ground cloves**

a pinch of **freshly grated nutmeg**

3 sprigs of **fresh thyme**, leaves only

2 tablespoons **finely chopped fresh mint**

2 tablespoons **finely chopped fresh parsley**

2 tablespoons **finely chopped fresh coriander**, plus extra to serve

1 slice of **stale bread**, soaked in milk until soft

fine salt

flatbreads, to serve

VEGETABLES:

2 **courgettes**, chopped into rough 3cm chunks

2 **red** or **yellow peppers**, seeded and chopped into rough 3cm chunks

16 **cherry tomatoes**, halved

4 teaspoons **pomegranate molasses**

2 tablespoons **olive oil**

These Middle Eastern meat patties are inspired by our much-eaten lamb kofta wrap.

Tahini is a paste made from sesame seeds, often used for hummus, and is well worth having in your storecupboard, along with tangy pomegranate molasses. Mixed with yoghurt, tahini makes a nutty, creamy moreish sauce.

SAUCE:

8 heaped tablespoons **yoghurt**

5 tablespoons **tahini**

lemon juice, to taste

Heat the oven to 200°C/400°F/gas mark 6. Place the lamb mince in a large bowl with the onion, garlic, spices, herbs, soaked bread and 1 teaspoon of fine salt. Use your hands to mix everything together, but stop once just combined – don't over-work the meat, as it will lose its texture and become chewy. Divide the mixture into 2 equal balls, then divide again and repeat until you have 16 equal pieces. Shape into 3cm × 6cm oblongs.

Tip the vegetables into a large ceramic dish – one big enough to fit all of them in a single layer (use two dishes if necessary). Add the pomegranate molasses, a pinch of salt and the oil and toss to coat. Arrange the vegetables and kofta in a single layer, so that they roast rather than stew in their own juices, and cook in the preheated oven for 30–35 minutes. The kofta should be cooked through and lightly browned on the outside. If the kofta are done before the vegetables, remove from the pan and keep warm while the vegetables cook for 5 or so minutes longer.

While the kofta are cooking, make the sauce: whisk together the yoghurt and tahini, then add a couple of teaspoons of lemon juice plus a little salt. Taste and add more lemon or salt as necessary. If the sauce is very thick, thin it with a tablespoon of cold water.

Serve the kofta and roasted vegetables on the flatbreads with the sauce, sprinkled with fresh coriander.

\\\\ TIP ////

To re-create LEON's kofta wrap,
roll your kofta up in a flatbread
with some chilli sauce, gem
lettuce, gherkins or dill pickles,
tomatoes, more fresh herbs and
some fresh pomegranate seeds.

HARISSA-BAKED CHICKEN & SWEET POTATOES

SERVES 2

PREP TIME: 10 MINS • COOK TIME: 45–60 MINS, plus 10 mins resting

WF

1 tablespoon **harissa paste**, or to taste

2 tablespoons **olive oil**

4 skin-on, bone-in **chicken thighs**

1 **red pepper**, seeded and roughly chopped into chunks

2 small or 1 very large **sweet potato**, sliced into 6 or 8 pieces

1 × 400g can of **chickpeas**, drained and rinsed (approx. 230g drained weight)

salt and **freshly ground black pepper**

TO SERVE:

fresh coriander

yoghurt or **soured cream**

A delicious, healthy, throw-together meal requiring very little attention until it is served.

Heat the oven to 180°C/350°F/gas mark 4.

First, taste the harissa: if yours is very spicy, use slightly less. Whisk the harissa and olive oil together. Place the chicken thighs in a roasting dish and add the red peppers and sweet potatoes, along with some salt and pepper. Pour over the harissa mixture and toss everything together.

Place the dish in the preheated oven and cook for 45–60 minutes, depending on the size of the thighs. Baste everything twice and turn the vegetables once, halfway through cooking.

Five minutes before the end of cooking, add the chickpeas to the pan to allow them to heat through cooking.

The chicken is cooked when the skin is golden and crisping up; check that the juices are running clear by piercing a thigh at the thickest point.

Remove from the oven and rest the meat for 5–10 minutes. Serve with fresh coriander and dollops of yoghurt or soured cream to offset the fiery harissa.

\\\\ TIP ////

Bigger appetites should go for whole chicken legs rather than thighs, in which case increase the cooking time by up to 10 minutes.

FISH IN CHRAIMEH SAUCE

SERVES 4

PREP TIME: 15 MINS • COOK TIME: 18 MINS

DF

1 tablespoon **olive oil**

6 cloves of **garlic**, finely chopped

4 heaped tablespoons **tomato purée**

1 **fresh red chilli**, seeded and
finely chopped

2 teaspoons **sweet paprika**

1 teaspoon **ground cumin**

2 heaped teaspoons **harissa**,
or more to taste

4 **roasted peppers** from a jar,
roughly chopped

2 tablespoons **lemon juice**

4 **fish fillets** or **fish steaks**
(**cod**, **salmon**, **hake**, **bass** or **trout**)

TO SERVE:
fresh coriander
fresh crusty bread

This chilli-spiked fish stew was created by Sephardic Jews in North Africa and then travelled to Israel, where it is hugely popular. It should be really fiery, so add more harissa if necessary.

Place the oil in a lidded pan large enough for all the fish fillets. Set over a medium heat and add the garlic. Let sizzle for 1 minute, stirring – don't allow it to burn. Add the tomato purée, chilli, paprika, cumin, harissa and red pepper pieces, and cook, stirring, for 2 minutes. Add just enough hot water to the pan to make the mixture saucy and simmer for 5 minutes. Taste and add more harissa if not spicy enough. Stir in the lemon juice.

Season the fish fillets, add to the pan and spoon the sauce over them. Turn the heat to low and cover with the lid. Cook until the fish is just done, about 8–10 minutes, depending on the thickness of the fish. Sprinkle with coriander and serve with plenty of crusty bread to mop up the spicy sauce.

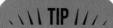

\\\ TIP ///

Instead of fish fillets, try using seafood. Make the sauce as above, then add cleaned live mussels or clams, raw prawns, squid, or a mixture, and cook for 3–4 minutes with the lid clamped on (discard any shells which haven't opened at the end of cooking). Or try adding butterbeans or haricots to the sauce as well as the fish.

HOT-SMOKED TROUT & WATERCRESS TART

SERVES 4 as a light meal
PREP TIME: 10 MINS • COOK TIME: 30 MINS

375g sheet of ready-rolled **puff pastry**, ideally all-butter

1 **egg**, beaten

1 heaped tablespoon **finely chopped fresh dill**

300g **full-fat crème fraîche**

zest of ½ **lemon**

2 teaspoons **wholegrain mustard** (optional)

300g **hot-smoked trout**, flaked into chunks

salt and **freshly ground black pepper**

a large handful of **watercress**, washed and thick stalks removed, to serve

A salad on a tart. In a good way.

Remove the pastry from the fridge 30 minutes before cooking. Heat the oven to 180°C/350°F/gas mark 4.

Line a large flat tray with greaseproof or baking paper. Lay the ready-rolled sheet of pastry on the paper. Score a border 1½cm from the edge of the pastry, using a sharp knife, then prick the middle of the pastry all over with a fork, taking care not to poke holes all the way through.

Brush the border with the beaten egg. Place the pastry in the preheated oven and cook for 10 minutes. The middle may puff up a little – if so, when you remove from the oven, let it cool slightly, then press gently to deflate it.

Mix the dill, crème fraîche, lemon zest, mustard and trout together, with a pinch of salt and lots of pepper, and spread the mixture evenly over the partially cooked pastry. Return to the oven for 20 minutes. When the base is golden and crisp, remove from the oven and strew with the watercress. Eat straight away.

\\\\ **TIP** ////
Any hot-smoked fish would work here. Don't be tempted to use lower fat crème fraîche, as it may split in the heat of the oven and curdle.

ASPARAGUS & TALEGGIO TART

SERVES 4 as a light meal

PREP TIME: 10 MINS • COOK TIME: 40 MINS

V

375g sheet of ready-rolled **puff pastry**, ideally all-butter

1 **egg**, beaten

3 **spring onions**, trimmed and finely diced

8 fat spears of **asparagus**, woody bases snapped off, cut in half lengthwise (if using thin spears, use 4 more and don't halve them)

3 teaspoons **olive oil**

200g **Taleggio**, cut into rough ½cm slices, then halved

salt and **freshly ground black pepper**

Sharp Taleggio cheese on buttery puff pastry with sweet asparagus.

Remove the pastry from the fridge 30 minutes before cooking. Heat the oven to 180°C/350°F/gas mark 4.

Line a large flat tray with greaseproof or baking paper. Lay the ready-rolled sheet of pastry on the paper. Score a border 1½cm from the edge of the pastry, using a sharp knife, then prick the middle of the pastry all over with a fork, taking care not to poke holes all the way through.

Brush the border with the beaten egg. Place the pastry in the oven and cook for 15 minutes. The middle may puff up a little – if so, when you remove from the oven, let it cool slightly, then press gently to deflate it.

Meanwhile, toss the vegetables with the olive oil and some salt and pepper. Top the partially cooked pastry with the cheese first, then add the spring onions and some black pepper. Return the tart to the oven for 15 minutes. Arrange the asparagus on top of the tart for a final 5–10 minutes. The tart is ready when the bottom is crisp and golden.

\\\\ TIP ////

Once you've nailed the puff tart technique, try making them with other semi-firm cookable cheeses like ricotta, feta or Stilton; or smoked salmon, chives and dill; even half-moons of chorizo with roasted red pepper.

BEETROOT, GOATS' CHEESE & WALNUT TART

SERVES 4 as a light meal

PREP TIME: 10 MINS • COOK TIME: 30 MINS

V

375g sheet of ready-rolled **puff pastry**, ideally all-butter

1 **egg**, beaten

200g **cooked beetroot** (not in vinegar), chopped into small wedges

2 **shallots**, very thinly sliced

25g **walnut pieces**

2 teaspoons **olive oil**

250g **goats' cheese**

3 sprigs of **fresh thyme**, leaves only

salt and **freshly ground black pepper**

Proper puff pastry is notoriously hard to make from scratch, but as long as you choose an all-butter version, you can buy excellent ready-made puff and keep it in the fridge or freezer for standby meals.

Choose a rindless soft goats' cheese if you prefer a gentler flavour; for something more robust, choose a cheese with a rind.

Remove the pastry from the fridge 30 minutes before cooking. Heat the oven to 180°C/350°F/gas mark 4.

Line a large flat tray with greaseproof or baking paper. Lay the ready-rolled sheet of pastry on the paper. Score a border 1½cm from the edge of the pastry, using a sharp knife, then prick the middle of the pastry all over with a fork, taking care not to poke holes all the way through.

Brush the border with the beaten egg. Place the pastry in the preheated oven and cook for 10 minutes. It may puff up a little – if so, when you remove from the oven, let it cool slightly, then press gently to deflate it.

Toss the beetroot and shallots in the oil.

Arrange everything except the walnuts on the partially cooked pastry, starting with the cheese, then the cooked beetroot and shallots – setting the oiled bowl aside – then add the thyme and some salt and freshly ground black pepper.

Return the tart to the oven for 15 minutes.

Toss the walnuts in the oiled bowl and scatter over the walnuts for a further 5 minutes cooking time. Serve warm.

4 PUFF PASTRY TARTS

CHEAT'S TARTE FLAMBÉE

SERVES 4 as a light meal
PREP TIME: 10 MINS · COOK TIME: 40 MINS

375g sheet of ready-rolled **puff pastry**, ideally all-butter

1 **egg**, beaten

300g **full-fat crème fraîche**

½ **small onion**, sliced into wafer-thin half-moons

100g **smoked pancetta** or **back bacon**, sliced into very thin matchsticks

freshly grated nutmeg

salt and **freshly ground black pepper**

Tartes flambées are from Alsace, and are usually made with a thin, yeasted dough a bit like pizza. But ready-made puff is just as tasty. This is inspired by the most famous tarte flambée, which involves wafer-thin slices of onion with matchsticks of smoky pancetta.

Remove the pastry from the fridge 30 minutes before cooking. Heat the oven to 180°C/350°F/gas mark 4.

Line a large flat tray with greaseproof or baking paper. Lay the ready-rolled sheet of pastry on the paper. Score a border 1½cm from the edge of the pastry, using a sharp knife, then prick the middle of the pastry all over with a fork, taking care not to poke holes all the way through.

Brush the border with the beaten egg. Place the pastry in the preheated oven and cook for 10 minutes. It may puff up a little – if so, when you remove from the oven, let it cool slightly, then press gently to deflate it.

Spread the crème fraîche over the partially cooked pastry, avoiding the borders. Season with salt and pepper, then scatter over the onion. Don't use all the onion if you don't need it – it should make a thin layer. Scatter over the chopped pancetta or bacon, then grate over a generous dose of nutmeg.

Return the tart to the oven for 20–30 minutes, checking it often, until the pancetta is cooked and the bottom of the pastry is crisp and golden.

\\\\ **TIP** ////
We love this with some sautéed wild mushrooms added, or shavings of Gruyère.

CHICKEN ROASTED WITH PRESERVED LEMONS & NEW POTATOES

SERVES 2

PREP TIME: 10 MINS • COOK TIME: 45 MINS, plus 5 mins resting

WF • GF • DF

2 whole **chicken legs**

200g **new potatoes**, halved

2 small **courgettes**, cut into large chunks

2 **preserved lemons**, flesh scraped out and discarded, peel sliced into wedges

2 tablespoons **olive oil**

2 sprigs of **fresh rosemary**

6 **cloves of garlic**, peeled and whole

1 **onion**, cut into wedges

salt and **freshly ground black pepper**

If you don't have (or like) preserved lemons, which have a powerful salty-citrus flavour, tuck a couple of wedges of fresh lemon in among the vegetables instead.

Heat the oven to 180°C/350°F/gas mark 4.

Place all the ingredients in a large roasting dish and toss together. Arrange in a single layer and place in the preheated oven. Cook for 45 minutes, turning the vegetables once and basting the chicken halfway through. If the vegetables are cooked and beginning to char, remove them from the tray, keep them warm, and return the chicken to the oven until the skin is golden and crisp.

Remove from the oven and leave the meat to rest for 5 minutes before serving.

SPANISH TORTILLA

SERVES 2

PREP TIME: 15 MINS • COOK TIME: 45 MINS, plus 2 mins standing

WF · GF · DF · V

· ·

180ml **olive oil**, plus 1 tablespoon

2 **onions**, sliced as finely as possible

500g **floury white potatoes**, peeled and sliced as finely as possible (ideally with a mandolin)

5 **eggs**

salt and **freshly ground black pepper**

The key to a great tortilla is that the layers of thinly sliced potato and onion are light rather than dense, and – crucially – it should have a hint of creamy, eggy wobble to its centre when you cut into it.

Don't worry about the apparently vast quantity of oil used here – most of it is drained away. You can add all sorts of extras when mixing in the eggs – try roasted peppers, cubes of chorizo, Spanish ham, cubes of melting cheese, feta, peas, cooked green beans, cooked asparagus or a mixture of any of the above.

· ·

Place 120ml of the oil in a medium-sized frying pan with a lid (ours is 25cm across), and set it over a low heat. When hot, add the sliced onions and potatoes plus a good pinch of salt, and use tongs or two wooden spoons to carefully toss everything in the oil. It will initially look rather cramped in the pan, but everything will wilt down and reduce. Pour the remaining 60ml of oil on top of the vegetables and cover with a lid.

Cook for about 35 minutes, gently tossing and turning everything about every 5 minutes. Then remove the lid, turn the heat up slightly, and cook, stirring often, so that the onions and potatoes colour ever so slightly.

Beat the eggs lightly in a large bowl until just combined. (Over-beating them will give the tortilla a spongy texture.) Season liberally with salt and black pepper. Once the vegetables are soft and a little golden, taste them to ensure that any raw flavours have completely disappeared. If so, use a slotted spoon to lift them from the pan, draining off the oil, and add to the bowl of eggs. Mix well.

Pour the oil out of the pan (cool and dispose of it; don't pour it down the sink). Wipe the pan out using kitchen paper, removing any dregs of potato, as the starch will make the tortilla stick. Wipe the edges too if any oil has dribbled out, so that it doesn't catch and burn later.

\\\\ TIP ////

If flipping the tortilla makes you nervous, slip it under a hot grill until just browned on top, but be very careful not to let it overcook.

Add a tablespoon of fresh oil to the pan and set over a low–medium heat. Pour the egg-and-potato mixture back into the pan, smooth the top over, and cook for 4½ minutes, until the egg is just beginning to set and look firm around the edges, and is turning golden brown on the bottom. While it is still very runny on top, place a plate with a rim over the pan and quickly invert it. Slide the tortilla back into the hot pan (this can get a bit messy; don't worry, it will neaten up as it cooks). Cook for another 2 minutes, just long enough to brown and set the underside. (Cook for slightly longer if you want the tortilla to be firm all the way through. You can check its level of done-ness by inserting the tip of a sharp knife.)

Remove the pan from the heat and slide the tortilla on to a clean serving plate. Leave to stand for a couple of minutes – it will continue to cook and firm up a little as it stands. Eat warm, sliced into wedges, or at room temperature.

PAN-FRIED GNOCCHI WITH TOMATO & BASIL

SERVES 3–4

PREP TIME: 8 MINS • COOK TIME: 15 MINS

WF · GF · (DF · V · Ve if not served with Parmesan)

3 tablespoons **olive oil**

1 × 500g packet of **ready-made gnocchi**

1 clove of **garlic**, whole but bruised

250ml good-quality **passata**

1 teaspoon **sherry vinegar** or **red wine vinegar**

1 tablespoon **extra virgin olive oil**

salt and **freshly ground black pepper**

TO SERVE:

freshly grated Parmesan (vegetarians should choose a vegetarian brand)

leaves from 4 sprigs of **fresh basil**, roughly torn or chopped

We admit it – this barely counts as cooking, but sometimes we all need this kind of meal: fast, family-friendly and absolutely fuss-free. Boiled potato gnocchi can be a bit sludgy and wet, but frying them gives them a golden crunchy shell.

One 500g packet of gnocchi might not be enough for 4 hungry adults, so add another 100g if you need to.

Place a wide frying pan over a medium–high heat and add the oil. When shimmering, carefully tip in the gnocchi and fry, turning often, until golden all over. Remove the gnocchi and set aside; keep them warm.

Turn the heat down slightly and add the garlic clove, to infuse its flavour into the oil. After a minute or two, add the passata and vinegar and simmer for a couple of minutes. Taste – most passata already contains salt, but add more if you need to. Season with black pepper. Remove from the heat and stir in the extra virgin olive oil. Remove the garlic clove. Drizzle the sauce over the warm, crisp gnocchi and serve with freshly grated Parmesan and basil on top.

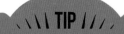

\\\ TIP ///

Instead of tomato sauce, try golden gnocchi with sautéed mushrooms, cream and thyme, or with bacon, peas and parsley.

INDEX

ABOUT THE AUTHORS

REBECCA SEAL

Rebecca has written about food and drink for the *Financial Times*, *Evening Standard*, the *Observer*, the *Guardian*, *Red* and *The Sunday Times*. Her cookbooks include *Istanbul: Recipes from the heart of Turkey* and *Lisbon: Recipes from the heart of Portugal*, as well as *LEON Happy Soups*, which she co-authored with John Vincent. She is one of the food and drink experts on Channel 4's *Sunday Brunch*. She believes that with the right skills, and just a bit of knowledge, everyone can eat well and hopes that her writing goes a little way towards helping that happen. She lives in London with her husband and two small daughters.

JOHN VINCENT

John Vincent is Co-founder of LEON, which now has more than 55 restaurants (including restaurants in Amsterdam, Utrecht, Oslo and Washington D.C). He wrote *LEON Naturally Fast Food* with Henry Dimbleby, *LEON Family & Friends* with Kay Plunkett-Hogge, *LEON Happy Salads* and *LEON Fast & Free* with Jane Baxter, and *LEON Happy Soups* with Rebecca Seal. He believes food has the power to delight, invigorate and bring people together – like him and Rebecca. He thinks that our relationship with food should be positive and joyous and that we need to listen more carefully to our gut, eat more good fats and less sugar. And a whole lot more plants.

ACKNOWLEDGEMENTS

REBECCA

Working with the team at LEON is always such a pleasure. I am really grateful for the chance to collaborate with John Vincent, and to be a small part of such a vibrant and interesting company. I'd like to thank Oliver Rowe, Elayna Rudolphy and Ella Tarn for working their food styling magic on the dishes, and making everything look wonderful. Alison Starling and Pauline Bache at Octopus make everything so easy, as does my agent, Antony Topping.

My youngest daughter, Coralie, was born in 2017, and I'm extremely thankful that she was such a mellow and chilled out baby so that I could work when she was still very little, to her big sister Isla for putting up with us turning her home into a photo studio (again), and to my parents Dave and Hilary Seal, for providing invaluable ad hoc childcare over and over again. I'm part of a local Whatsapp group, called the Secondtime Mums, and they helped keep me sane while juggling kids and work, as well as giving me recipe ideas and popping by with tupperware to relieve the pressure on my freezer. Thanks to Rinku Dutt for letting me use her delicious recipe on page 150, too.

My husband Steve took the beautiful pictures in the book. This is our fifth book, and working together just keeps getting better and better.

JOHN

I bow down to Rebecca who has again not only showed herself to be the most talented and hard working cook and food writer, but also the most wonderful human being. Surely, somewhere, there must be a dark side to you Rebecca. I just can't find it. You are positive, sunny, committed, courageous, kind, and you seem to have no ego. Thank you for being my co-author and for the adventure we are sharing. Thank you to Steve for being the live-in photographer again – you and Rebecca are a dream team. Jo Ormiston has worked with me now at LEON for four years and has been an important part of our growth. Thank you Jo.

Leon is named after my Dad. He deserves a thank you for the lifetime of inspiration he has given me. You are the funniest and cleverest man I know. My mum Marion, a teacher in every sense, and still teaching in schools at 81, keeps our family life together when Katie and I are a little too busy (which is most of the time). Mum we owe you so much. Those who know Mum will know I am not exaggerating when I say that you are the most positive and considerate person most people will ever have the privilege of knowing. Thank you to Katie, my wife, who is my hero. And to Natasha and Eleanor, I won't embarrass you here (I'll do that elsewhere like I normally do) but I would like to say 'porridge' and 'sugar'.

Everything good that happens at LEON, all the adventures and successes, come from the hard work of the team members who make and serve our food every day. Thank you so much to all of you, and to the managers (aka 'Mums and Dads') who support you every day.

An Hachette UK Company
www.hachette.co.uk

First published in Great Britain in 2018 by Conran Octopus,
an imprint of Octopus Publishing Group Ltd
Carmelite House
50 Victoria Embankment
London EC4Y 0DZ
www.octopusbooks.co.uk

ISBN 978-1-84091-772-7

A CIP catalogue record for this book is available from the British Library.
Printed and bound in Italy

10 9 8 7 6 5 4 3 2 1

Photography by Steven Joyce

Publisher: Alison Starling
Design, art direction and styling: Jo Ormiston
Styling assistants: Elayna Rudolphy and Ella Tarn
Food styling: Oliver Rowe
Creative director: Jonathan Christie
Senior editor: Pauline Bache
Copyeditor: Annie Lee
Senior production manager: Katherine Hockley

We have endeavoured to be as accurate as possible in all the
preparation and cooking times listed in the recipes in this book.
However they are an estimate based on our own timings during recipe
testing, and should be taken as a guide only, not as the literal truth.

Nutrition advice is not absolute. If you feel you require consultation
with a nutritionist, consult your GP for a recommendation.

Standard level spoon measurements are used in all recipes.
1 tablespoon = one 15ml spoon
1 teaspoon = one 5ml spoon

Eggs should be medium unless otherwise stated and preferably
free range and organic. The Department of Health advises that eggs
should not be consumed raw. This book contains dishes made with
raw or lightly cooked eggs. It is prudent for more vulnerable people
such as pregnant and nursing mothers, invalids, the elderly, babies
and young children to avoid uncooked or lightly cooked dishes made
with eggs. Once prepared these dishes should be kept refrigerated
and used promptly.

Fresh herbs should be used unless otherwise stated. If unavailable use
dried herbs as an alternative but halve the quantities stated.

Ovens should be preheated to the specific temperature – if using a
fan-assisted oven, follow manufacturer's instructions for adjusting the
time and the temperature.

This book includes dishes made with nuts and nut derivatives. It is
advisable for customers with known allergic reactions to nuts and
nut derivatives and those who may be potentially vulnerable to these
allergies, such as pregnant and nursing mothers, invalids, the elderly,
babies and children, to avoid dishes made with nuts and nut oils. It is
also prudent to check the labels of pre-prepared ingredients for the
possible inclusion of nut derivatives.

Vegetarians should look for the 'V' symbol on a cheese to ensure it is
made with vegetarian rennet. There are vegetarian forms of Parmesan,
feta, Cheddar, Cheshire, Red Leicester, dolcelatte and many goats'
cheeses, among others.

Not all soy sauce is gluten-free – we use tamari (a gluten-free type of
soy sauce), but check the label if you are unsure.

Remember to check the labels on ingredients to make sure they don't
have hidden refined sugars. Even savoury goods can be artificially
sweetened so it's always best to check the label carefully.